Voices in the Wilderness

By Ron Morehead

i

Copyright Information

Voices in the Wilderness (Second Edition)
Copyright © 2013 Ron Morehead
All Rights Reserved

Library of Congress
Cataloging-in-Publication Data

Morehead, Ronald J.,

Self-Published by Ron Morehead

Paperback book is printed in USA

ISBN: 978-0-9851151-3-5

The Digital eBook, The Bigfoot Recordings and other products may be ordered on our website:
http://www.bigfootsounds.com/store
http://www.bigfoot-sounds.com/store.html

OR

by Direct Mail at:

Sierra Sounds
P.O. Box 2248
Mariposa, CA 95338

Cover art by:
Scott Curtis
http://www.truthful-solutions.com

Dedication

AL BERRY
1941-2012

Without whom this book would not have been written.

CD Sleeve

Voices In The Wilderness
Audio Tracks for the Book

Track		Track	
#1	Test	#13	Question?
#2	Disagreement	#14	Appala Question
#3	First Recording	#15	Child's Play
#4	Whistle Exchange	#16	Sightings
#5	Breathing	#17	Toilet Seat Bang
#6	Berry Recording	#18	Light Shine
#7	Limb	#19	Whoop Interaction
#8	Rocks	#20	Samurai
#9	Rhythmic	#21	Humaya Poya
#10	Whoops	#22	Smacking
#11	Talking To Us?	#23	Fast Talk
#12	Humorous?	#24	Ohio Sound

Sierra Sounds™

Table of Contents

Acknowledgments

My sincere gratitude to the many people who helped with this book; to all those who provided support, read, wrote, offered comments, allowed me to quote their remarks and assisted in the editing, proofreading and design.

Above all I thank my dear friend Chris Meda for her unwavering support, her inspiration, and encouragement toward this project by providing her tireless proofreading and suggestions.

Many thanks to Alan Berry who, unknowingly, taught me much about professionalism, the Kings English, and fly-fishing. He passed away in January of 2012. He was a good friend throughout the years; we share a lot of memories and have had many thought-provoking conversations around numerous campfires.

My warmest appreciation to Tom Yamarone and Christopher Noel for their reliable input with the editing. Also contributing to this book's editing were Sarah Brewster, Gunnar Monson, Carolyn Matthews, Judy Locke, and Dr. Jim Upton. I also appreciate their very professional help.

A special thanks to Peter Byrne for 'trying' to keep me in the middle and on track.

For their contribution, I have the utmost respect and appreciation for Joe Hauser, Nancy Logan, R. Scott Nelson and Professor R. Lynn Kirlin for sticking their professional neck out and providing their unbiased expertise.

Appreciation to Scott Curtis for his excellent talent in preparing the cover.

And, to Bill Hilton Jr., for his expertise in preparing the eBook and his long-lasting friendship. http://www.truthful-solutions.com

To my very special friend, Bill McDowell, who is like a brother to me and helped with my memory about those earlier times at our Sierra camp, I say, "Thanks" for the years of friendship and all the great memories that go with them.

Lastly, my children: I am very grateful to each of them for their encouragement; Ronika, Rhonda, Rachelle and Royce, each of whom shared their experiences and thoughts toward this project. I am so very proud of them all.

Prologue

A few thousand years ago people thought that a solar eclipse suggested that God must have put his hand over the sun. It wasn't until the 1500's when it was determined the earth was actually round and moved around the sun, and then folks became a little smarter. Can humans get smarter now? Can we discover something maybe more profound, something that challenges even the brightest of minds? With evidence licking its chops in the face of classical scientists, will they (can they) acknowledge another unique primate, one that might be beyond their disciplinary realm? An enigmatic primate referred to as Bigfoot.

How do we explain the hundreds of reports that associate Bigfoot with paranormal activity? There is a common denominator, and it's not necessarily supernatural...just not completely understood. It takes us beyond classical science and moves us into another science that is usually kept in the closet. Accepted worldwide, Quantum Physics hasn't been considered by many to have anything to do with the Bigfoot phenomenon. Why not? How far down this 'Rabbit Hole' can we go?

With pictures, data, and creature vocalizations, Ron Morehead takes you on a journey through his 40-year chronicle that will drop you down that Rabbit Hole; examining the nature of these mysterious creatures. Your journey begins at a remote hunting camp in the rugged Sierra Nevada Mountains of California where a family of Bigfoots raucously began to harass Ron and his hunting buddies.

Thinking of Bigfoot as a unique backwoods undiscovered ape is an understatement. Ron thought then, but has verified now, that they are self-aware, have language, and are probably much, much more. After sharing his personal experiences he provides you with the evidence that might drop a jaw or two. Yes, in a unique way, he also gives his personal opinion about what they are; suggesting why they are here, and what their purpose could be. Maybe he's having his own eclipse of the mind, but his story has held up, having been time-tested by science and is very compelling. But, you can decide.

In this book Ron provides a hypothesis that can allow you to connect the dots and get a picture of what Bigfoot could actually be...a picture that might cause you to 'pause' and possibly have a very 'guarded' approach when coming in contact with these giants who stealthily linger in the shadows.

Foreword

In medical terms, stories regarding patients are called "Case Histories" and are often cited in journals to highlight an unexpected medical result, which may even suggest a new and different therapy that may need more scientific study.

This story by Ron Morehead is about his encounters around the Sasquatch/Bigfoot beings, but it's more than just a "case history". Here, in this book, we now have the best factual observations ever gathered, chronologically arranged and scientifically supported, for the benefit of all current or future researchers of this enigma. From his first trip into this remote region of the Sierra Mountains of California to his most recent one, Ron takes the reader through an impressive history that provides the context by which actual recorded vocalizations of the Sasquatch were documented.

This book is more than just a fleeting, single encounter with a Sasquatch, but rather an on-going set of encounters with a family of these giants. And also unlike almost every other Sasquatch encounter, Ron's constellation of events comes with an impressive body of physical evidence. Remarkably, this book represents and unprecedented 'case history' of encounters that spans a forty-year period. In contrast with most other accounts, this book also comes with an array of audio recordings that have been carefully scrutinized and endorsed by science and multiple professionals who are well credentialed in linguistics and audiology. As "case histories" go, Ron's history is as good as it gets.

I have seen and heard Ron speak at a few different conferences over the years. I have pored over copies of his remarkable recordings. But, until now I have never had the chance to read the entire, carefully written chronology of events that transpired over his forty years in this wilderness habitat. Ron's landmark book provides the Sasquatch enthusiast and the scientific community with the most credible case history of a long-term encounter between a group of humans and a group of Sasquatches ever published.

As a researcher and devotee of all things Sasquatch, most of what I do is to look for patterns. By applying the laws of statistics and probability to uncertain events, one can actually apply a measure of science to the seemingly unscientific body of sighting-report data. I agreed to write this foreword because, after reading Ron's accounts, I was impressed with how consistent those accounts were with the numerous other situations

I have studied. His descriptions fit the patterns I have assembled to a tee, and on that basis, I can state with absolute confidence that his claims of Sasquatch encounters are utterly true. I don't think they will, or can, ever be disproven and in fact, I predict they will ultimately become the standard by which all future long-term witness claims will be judged.

When I reflect on my own learning curve, I think of the years I spent figuring out what the patterns were. Had Ron's descriptions been available to me earlier, he would have saved me a decade of time spent figuring these things out for myself.

Thom Powell

Thom Powell
Author of 'The Locals' & 'Shady Neighbors'

Preface

A few years ago, with the encouragement of Al Berry, the investigative reporter who was invited to our remote camp, I began presenting my account about Bigfoot "publicly" in conferences and symposiums.   Al had written his story in a 1976 Bantam Book, entitled *Bigfoot*, but the whole story (my story) had not been told.   At that time I lived in a small community and was known as a successful businessman.   I became emboldened – at least I didn't 'see' or hear the locals laugh when I talked about Bigfoot. Actually, some of the folks came out of their closet and privately told me about sighting or encounters they had – one being a deputy sheriff.

Although Al told his story in his book, it was from his perspective as an investigator.   In 2008, inspired by a Crypto-Linguistic study, which established a complex language within the sounds we recorded, it became apparent that a more thorough, up-to-date, written chronicle of the events should be made available.   Therefore, I've written this book.

My story spans 40 years of exploration into the wilds of the Sierra Nevada Mountains of California – attempting to solve the mysteries that surround these giants who have remained extremely enigmatic.   I've also travelled extensively, interviewing folks that claim encounters, and have coupled some of the more credible accounts together with my own experiences. Thus, I think I've established a profile which is frank, honest, and hopefully helpful to others.   However, it may only be helpful if one has an open mind and is not "fixated" upon a predetermined paradigm.

The topic of Bigfoot is controversial – do they really exist? Yes, they do. I know this because I've been amongst them, trying to trick them, expose them, and most of all, trying to get a good picture – any kind of picture. After many attempts of "trying", it became apparent that these creatures have the ability to reason and figure things out. In retrospect, had I known what I know now, I would have taken much better care of the opportunity that existed when they must have felt "okay" to openly interact with us humans – and in a very close-up way.

Perhaps other folks, when armed with this knowledge, and are presented with the same opportunity, will handle their Bigfoot circumstance better. Understanding what I and the other hunters have gone through to find out more about them, should encourage and promote a better way for folks to explore this phenomenon.

The on-line book has either embedded sounds or links to those sounds – the hard copy book includes a CD. Writing my story, and including actual Bigfoot vocalizations, has obviously never been done before – there is a lot more to it than just writing the story. Others were involved, editing, proofing, PC guru, graphics, layout, etc., and I appreciate the input that each gave. Please take the time to review those contributors on the 'Acknowledgments' page.

Ron Morehead

See Pg. 124 "About The Author Page"

Peter Byrne
Statement

R on Morehead's new book, *Voices in the Wilderness*, is a fine contribution to the present-day mass of writing on the Bigfoot mystery. More than that, it is also very different in that its basic theme is a quite extraordinary aspect of the phenomenon...a series of vocalizations that professional analysis suggests may well be the only known example that we have of the possibility of language on the part of the creatures.

The source of these sounds - a group of the creatures that on several occasions visited Ron's camp in the High Sierras of northern California - has been adequately documented by Ron and his associates and a considerable part of the book contains accounts of the long and many hours of field work that he and his field workers put in to obtaining them and to meticulously recording them. The results, as detailed in his book, are quite extraordinary - indeed unique - in the history of the phenomenon and in what many of us call The Great Search.

So fascinating and so different are they that their credibility - as is to be expected – has been challenged by researchers working in the phenomenon. So far, no one has been able to disprove their authenticity and part of the reason for this may well be due to the high esteem in which Ron and his small group of co-workers are held and, in addition, the impeccable integrity which he, and they, have applied to the work.

Readers of his new book will find this integrity a theme that runs all the way through his writing - and his findings - providing them with an undeniably solid foundation. The result...is highly persuasive reading for anyone with even a glimmer of interest in the Bigfoot phenomenon and in the perplexing questions that it imposes on us as one of the last great mysteries of planet earth.

Peter Byrne

Author of:
The Search for Bigfoot
Gone are the Days
Hunting in the Mountains & Jungles of Nepal
Gentleman Hunter
Tula Hati
Monster Trilogy

Al Berry
Statement

In this book, Ron Morehead has recounted his adventures high up in the Sierras playing a sort of cat and mouse game with what at once seems to be a flesh and blood, human-like creature – yet maybe not, for its vocalization is virtually inimitable to scientists. It doesn't seem to want to harm anybody and is very curious about its more urban-suburban variants in primate land.

Ron and I became acquainted during one of these brushes in 1972 at a hunter's camp and have been fast friends ever since. We always hope that somewhere on the lonely backwoods trail or along the Sierra ridge tops we would finally bump into one of these things full face, and come away with a prize photo showing that there is another primate in this world beside ourselves to wonder about.

We've had many discussions about our encounters in the Sierras; what are they, how do they do the things they do, and why? A number of years ago in an overnight camp, we joined the company of some locals who thought they had encountered a strange creature. There were several of us, including some young bucks who thought they knew everything, until a fist-size rock whizzed above our heads at the fire pit and smacked into a tall cedar at a height of 20 feet. I had my .45 caliber pistol in hand (only time I've ever drawn it this side of Vietnam) because that rock chipped off a chunk of cedar bark 12 inches long by 4 inches wide, and if the rock had instead hit somebody, it could have injured or killed him.

The encounters I most enjoyed (and shivered about afterward) were at the high Sierra camp. We tried everything to get our jib-jabbering friends to show themselves. There were moments of promise, but 1972 passed with no results, other than that which we recorded. I have deeply embedded wonderments that go back to those early encounters: How do they come and go with such ease...I mean disappear and re-appear, leaving their footprints about?

Alan Berry
Author:
Bigfoot, Bantam, 1976
XO, A Soldier's Story Written in 2011

Introduction

This book is about the experiences of a man who witnessed, recorded, and had vocal interactions between himself and a family of giants, commonly referred to as Bigfoot or Sasquatch.* His story is true and begins in 1971 when he, along with a group of five other hunters, encountered these creatures in a remote and imposing part of the Sierra Nevada mountains of California. It spans his 40-year history trekking in-and-out of this secluded area to seek out and understand the enigmas associated with these beings. What makes his story so different and compelling is not only the supporting documentation but the recurrent effort on the part of these "beings" to communicate with this group of hunters. In this book the author has included a CD with actual recorded interactions. It also provides the context in which they were made. When the "Track Number" appears, the reader can play that sound on the CD. The eBook has embedded sound tracks or links to those tracks.

Challenged by skeptics, but time-tested by science, this account brings to the reader an exciting report of unsurpassed vocal interaction between humans and Bigfoot. This book is meant to encourage the Bigfoot enthusiast, direct him or her to those techniques that worked for the author, and to inspire those who still believe we humans have a lot to learn about nature and the cosmos.

Science has established that these unusual sounds were spontaneous and made at the time of the recordings. And, in a more recent study, a complex language was discovered. The author thinks they are self-aware and, like humans, can reason using cognizant thought. From a shrewd forest monster to a half-human remnant of a demigod, the reader should be prepared for an exclusive look at what this author thinks. His story also provides the reader with a unique and refreshing insight into the nature of these giants.

But, what exactly are these legendary beings that stealthily roam the forest? Why did they choose to interact with this man and this particular group of hunters? What do they want to convey?

Voices in the Wilderness

"Something eerie had been stalking our hunting camp. Without warning, and on its own terms, that 'something' would seize the night and jar us with ape-like noises. Those enormous sounds could almost shake the walls of our protective log shelter. But on this particular night, we were outside those questionably 'protective walls' when it started up. Never had this unknown visitor been so out-and-out bold. It was then that Bill and I knew we were in for a night of it."

Chapter 1

Invitation to Adventure

Track #1 - Test Recording

S haron had been told not to talk about it, but her husband might be in big trouble – life-threatening trouble. If she went to the authorities, they'd surely laugh at her. But she had to talk to someone, and it was me. "Have you ever heard of Bigfoot?" she asked. Her bothered look got my attention. I knew her husband, Bill, was gone and was part of a closed circle of hunters that packed into a remote place in the Sierra Nevada Mountains to look for deer. "I was raised in Northern California where the Bigfoot creature was supposedly filmed," I said. The 1967 Patterson-Gimlin film had made headlines in the local paper and got a lot of attention. But aside from my short-lived interest in that film, I knew nothing.

It was hunting season in September of 1971. She went on to tell me that he and his buddies should have been back by now and that a couple of members of the group recently experienced some very weird and unfamiliar animal sounds at their camp. That statement troubled me, too. The McDowells had become good friends to my wife and me, and our children had begun to mix quite well. Bill was a contractor and I a restaurateur. We also served together as board members of a large church in Merced, California.

Because of the unknown source of the sounds and the horrific story told to them by the Johnson brothers, all the wives were worried. The next day when Donald, Bill's brother-in-law, asked me to join him for a hike to the camp, my adrenalin surged and I jumped at the chance. Donald's account of this high-country retreat, coupled with the concern in his eyes, elevated my interest even more. To say the least, he was uneasy and seemed troubled about making the trip alone. A few days earlier while staying in camp for the first time that year, he had a very frightening experience involving these 'things' of the night. He fled the camp when daybreak came, leaving only a note for the others to read. Whatever was sounding off and stalking the guys at night wasn't anything he ever wanted to experience again. His religious beliefs were temporarily in shambles. "Man" was supposed to be the dominant creature on this earth and these "things" — whatever they were — scared the hell out of him, if there was any.

What could it be? When Donald first heard the story from Warren and Louis Johnson, he figured it had to be a rogue bear — nothing else made sense to him. But, experiencing these powerful and very threatening displays during the night was all it took to drive him off that mountain. By now, they considered Bigfoot as the source of the sounds. That it was not a "known, predictable animal" made it all the more frightening to Donald.

The unknown has always fascinated me and this seemed to be one of those mysteries that just could be one of the bigger jewels in the remaining pile of earthly unknowns. The Patterson-Gimlin film was just a pale memory in the back of my mind. Could it actually have been real? Could this be real? I knew Bill and he was not one given to whims or irrational assumptions. If Bill and the other hunters were really in trouble, I wanted to help. And if this story was real, I wanted to be part of it. Either way, I was in.

*The creature inframe 352 was estimated to be 7'3 1/2" tall,
with an approximate waist of 72" and a weight of 500 lbs.*

An accurate spatial reference has been established from research photographs taken by Peter Byrne of Rich Hodgson in 1972 at the Bluff Creek Site. Hodgson, with footwear, is 6' 1 3/4" and weighs 165 lbs. and has a 32" waist.

Just before daybreak Donald and I left the warmth of our San Joaquin Valley homes, and after a few hours of driving into the mountains, we were finally at the trailhead – it was time to walk. My adrenaline began to surge. I didn't know if we were on a rescue mission, a vigorous hike, or maybe a one-way trip. I didn't ask and he didn't volunteer to tell me how much hiking we'd need to do. He obviously didn't want to discourage the one who agreed to join him on this trek into the wilderness where these "whatevers" lingered in the shadows. But with a little "heads-up" I would have drank a bit more coffee that morning. The sudden change in elevation from the valley floor to this high-country region took away the "oomph" in my muscles and gave my lungs, and thought-to-be-good physique, an early morning jerk. All he said when we began was, "This is gonna' be a little tug."

As we started the hike, my thoughts raced. At any other time a bird whizzing by wouldn't be a big deal. But on this trip the shadowy trees seemed to have something peering from behind them. I think my eyes were getting red from not blinking, but after an hour or so my attention changed. My muscles began burning as we continued up the brutal switch-backs of the trail. Slowly my legs began to give way to the feeling of Jell-O and I think my wheezing must have become audible to Donald. Hoping for a pause to take a breather and look around, I asked, "How much farther?" As we continued, no matter how many times I asked, his reply was the same; "Ah, we're gettin' closer, but we got a ways more to go." Once or twice he asked if I was okay. "I'm good," I gasped. As crazy as it may sound, the thought of having a brush with these unknown creatures was unquestionably driving my body. No way did I want to admit that I was becoming exhausted. Donald, a hard worker who had made the trip many times over the years, was like a veteran mule.

The trailhead began at 6,400 feet elevation. The first two miles up that mountain was the biggest challenge. After about another mile or so, we left the main trail and then there wasn't a trail at all. We climbed to over 10,000 feet and continued the trek down one canyon, up another, across ravines and through creeks pushing alder and brush out of our way. Donald said that the guys usually took different routes so that other hunters or hikers would be less likely to see their tracks and stumble onto their old hunting camp. "That could mess up the deer supply," he said.

Sierra Nevada Mountains

Runs 400 miles (644 km) north-to-south, and is approximately 70 miles (113 km) across east-to-west. Mount Whitney at 14,505 feet (4,421 m), the highest point in the contiguous United States.

Besides the occasional glance up, looking for some type of monster, my view wasn't on the trail, but of my hands pushing my knees which helped my burning leg muscles. I must have been following Donald too close. On occasions, a branch would slap me in the head. That seemed to knock the slack out and kept me going...I'm still not sure if Donald meant to do that.

We arrived at camp that afternoon only to find the guys were okay and were packing to leave. They were visibly shaken from the prior nights' sounds, yet no monster was seen and nobody was eaten. They'd spent a couple extra nights, with pistols fully loaded, huddled inside the shelter – trying to keep their composure. They thought at any moment 'something' was coming through those log walls. Bill gave me a quick tour of the camp area and led me to an 18-inch five-toed bare foot impression. That print with splayed toes was impressive and, as tired as I was, I wanted to see more. But there was little daylight remaining, and the men were in a hurry.

The thought of leaving the area right away didn't make me want to jump up and down for joy – assuming I could have. Deer carcasses were packed, camp was secured, and it was past time to get on the trail. There's more downhill trekking getting out of that area, which makes the trip a lot less time-consuming than going in. Bill may have noticed how I was stumbling over nothing and asked if I wanted to ride Eagle, his roan horse. I thought about it for about two seconds and said, "Okay." Eagle was a big, strong horse and my muscle-tightened legs didn't want to put my boots into the stirrups. But when I finally made it into the saddle I began to think, "It feels good to actually sit and have four legs under me that do all the walking...horses can be a good thing." Eagle took me all the way out.

The trip in and out of that camp was a real eye-opener for me. I hadn't known an unspoiled spot like that existed. As a private pilot I knew there was a lot of wilderness in that vast mountain range, but I hadn't seen it from this new perspective. The caliber of the men, the well-preserved area, and just the sheer excitement of the unknown had suddenly, but surely, introduced me to another world.

18" Non-human impression next to human

Author holding 18" cast

Author packing in the high country

Chapter 2

First Contact

(Warren and Louis Johnson)

It was the month before hunting season when Warren and Louis decided to make a summer trek to their remote camp. By doing so, the brothers were able to see what damage the bears may have done to the shelter and would also assess the deer population. The winter's heavy snow and/or perhaps bears rummaging will generally take a toll on the camp and it's always fun to look for deer. These were great reasons for a brisk hike into this beautiful region of the Sierra Nevada Mountains of California. But, absolutely nothing could have prepared the Johnsons for the experience they were about to have.

Warren Johnson was the group's leader, and also the general manager of a large San Joaquin Valley business near Modesto, California. He and his brother Louis had been hunting this area since the late 50's and knew it like the back of their hands. In their minds, a Bigfoot-like creature was a myth, not an actual being – not 'til now anyway, when the 'myth turned into reality'. While in this mountainous getaway their attention was taken from their busy lives in the valley and was comfortably coupled with the serenity of this high country region. They both took pride in this primitive, backwoods spot and it clearly showed in their mannerisms and the way the camp was organized. They considered this wilderness environment a kind of 'private sanctuary' and really didn't want anyone messing it up.

Both brothers kept an arsenal of rifles and handguns at their homes, and actually loaded their own ammunition with the exact amount of powder for the best results. Later, after I'd been around these guys more, I realized that they were really good hunters – actually not just good, but excellent. On one occasion, I witnessed Warren shoot a deer from about a 1,000 yards away – clear across a canyon. One shot, one kill. Anyone can get lucky, but while I was watching the deer fall through my binoculars another came into view just a few feet away from the first, and 'boom', Warren did it again.

While hunting on another occasion, I arrived back at camp before the others. Immediately I heard something crashing down the ridge through the woods. There it was, a really nice buck bouncing right toward me. It had been a long day and I hadn't shot anything yet – this could be my chance. I quickly raised my rifle to take aim when a shot rang out. The hackneyed phrase, "If you snooze, you lose," is probably appropriate – I was just too slow on the draw. The deer dropped, tumbling head over hooves into camp. There it was, lying at my feet, when Warren appeared. He shot the deer on the run, but had been patiently stalking it, waiting 'til it got closer to camp. "I didn't want to drag him too far," Warren said.

Sierra Camp Shelter

Louis was just as good a hunter and after a while I realized just how exceptional their other outdoor skills were, too. They seemed to be extremely fine-tuned to this unspoiled wilderness. Warren and Louis always carried handguns with them to camp, and only brought rifles during hunting season. Clearly the Johnson brothers were the 'hunters'

12

hunters'. I've witnessed unbelievable shots by these guys. One time a humming bird was zipping around, in and out, interrupting their afternoon nap, when Warren told Louis, "I'll shoot him, if you'll eat him?" That may sound a bit morbid, but the challenge was answered. Warren pulled out his .44 caliber magnum and from a respectable distance, shot the bird, while it was flying. Not much of a meal remained, but Louis did keep his part of the bargain.

But, completely aside from their shooting ability, the trip to camp in August of 1971 was life-altering for the Johnson brothers. One evening, after they ate their dinner and went into the shelter, they heard crashing and banging outside. Whatever began to interrupt their rest was wrecking their stove area, and the huge sounds were a real sleep-stopper, unlike anything they'd ever heard in the past fifteen years they'd been going there.

At first Warren thought it might be the big bear that he'd seen the previous year. He grabbed his flashlight and started to go out to scare it off. * He had just started opening the door when the sounds outside changed his mind. He heard deep guttural grunts, snarls and what sounded like teeth-popping. There was also the sound of chest-beating. Occasionally, it sounded like two creatures in violent disagreement. This went on for a half hour.**

Play Soundtrack (2) **Taped later in the year.

Shortly after the sounds stopped, they took their flashlights and cautiously slipped out of the shelter's opening. The pots and pans were scattered, the leftover Spam was gone, and two 18 3/4-inch five-toed, human-like footprints were in the mud. Their hearts pumped faster as their jaws dropped. They knew whatever had been making those noises had to be much, much bigger than they were.

They immediately rushed back into the shelter, and roped the log opening shut with a heavy nylon rope. They didn't get much sleep that night. The next morning they took pictures of the tracks to document what had happened the previous night, "We just wanted to make sure it wasn't caused by something we ate," Warren said. They took a hike and spent a lot of time that day looking over their shoulders. Curiosity, coupled with confidence in their survival skills, overcame their anxiety to leave and they

*Summarizing from Warren Johnson's notes

decided to stick it out another night. Although they didn't know what type of animal they were dealing with, they each knew how to handle a gun and where to target an aggressive animal if they were attacked.

Warren also thought one of the creatures may have been burned the previous evening by a teapot full of hot water left on the stove and become angry. He figured some type of bad attitude was required to support those scary sounds and the wrecking of the stove area.

On the second night the brothers rigged up a food trap. They cooked some bacon and carefully stacked empty tin cans on top of the skillet so that when the bait was taken the cans would fall and they'd know something was there. They also left out a pitcher of punch. This time when they went into the shelter they left the doorway open. The plan was to rush out with their flashlights to try and get a look at whatever it was.

It happened, but the visitor was too fast – way too fast. All they saw was a glimpse of a shadowy figure crashing through the thick alders by the spring. What type of animal could move that fast? All the bacon was gone and the punch, too.

The empty punch container was sitting almost exactly where it was and not a drop appeared to have been spilled. Their speedy, opportunistic eater escaped and still remained unidentified. The brothers went back into the shelter thinking it was over for the night, but they were wrong. Within five minutes the powerful voices came back and began to make sounds just like the night before.

With pistols cocked and loaded, every ear-throbbing moment for the Johnson brothers was like an eternity. Whatever was making those powerful sounds and leaving those huge tracks could easily crash through the walls of their primitive shelter. Would handguns stop it? Again, they endured the night, but the next morning they secured camp and hiked out.

This trip, however, was the start of many sleepless nights at the camp, often with frustrating encounters, but also the beginning of an unsurpassed adventure. Warren and Louis' thoughts toward this predictable campsite had changed; their attitudes and beliefs were challenged by these events and the likelihood that they *had* actually encountered the legendary Bigfoot was real.

Warren Johnson, Bill McDowell, Louis Johnson

Chapter 3

Contact for Help

Warren and Louis returned in a few days with a cassette tape recorder, purposely left food out for the creatures and ended up recording the very first vocalizations from these huge strangers of the night.

Play Soundtrack (3)

These unusual goings-on were followed by several others that year and we all began to take recorders with us to camp. Warren thought the story should be disclosed to someone that might believe in the existence of these creatures and not just shun the account as the product of a colorful imagination. He was an executive who had maintained a high degree of integrity in his community and felt the need to protect his local reputation. He would only share the story with a few close friends and asked the rest of us to do the same. He felt the camp's location should be cautiously guarded and information about this new 'unknown' should be kept away from the public for now. But he also felt something defining needed to be done to try and get to the bottom of the enigma.

Warren wrote a lengthy letter to Dr. Ivan T. Sanderson, founder of the Society for the Investigation of the Unexplained, detailing the events that had been taking place at the camp. Dr. Sanderson forwarded Warren's letter to Peter Byrne, a widely recognized Bigfoot researcher in northern Oregon. Peter's colorful background as the first professional big game hunter and safari guide in Nepal was well known, as well as his many expeditions to establish the existence of the Yeti in the Himalaya. As intriguing as the story sounded, California's Sierra Nevada mountain range was considered out of Peter's area of research. His funding limited him to the Oregon and Washington area.

Al Berry and Peter Byrne, 1975

Peter contacted Alan Berry, a reporter working for the Redding Record Searchlight newspaper, in Redding, California. Peter asked Al if he had time to interview the hunters regarding this report. Warren's account was thought unbelievable at the time, considered to be a hoax, and it was assumed that somebody was pulling someone's chain. After calling Warren, however, Al made the trip to Modesto to meet with the group. He interviewed each hunter separately and listened to the cassette recordings that were captured at camp that year.

The interviews, coupled with their story, were compelling enough for him to give this matter some serious attention. That winter of 1971, after discussing the issue with the others, Warren invited Al to visit the camp. But he had to wait until the snow melted next summer. If this was a hoax, Al was determined to uncover it.

Chapter 4

Greenhorn's Trip to Camp

The group's thoughts and feelings toward the camp had changed. It wasn't just a pristine distant hunting retreat now. It had taken on a whole new persona, one of adventure and excitement – one shrouded in mystery, and I became part of it.

Discussions about this camp and the unusual presence of these 'unknowns' seemed to be all Bill and I talked about when we were together. During the fall of 1971, after a few more trips with Bill, my lungs got used to the lighter air, and my leg muscles tightened up. I knew the way in and, perhaps more importantly, the way out.

It was time to evaluate and prioritize what I thought I wanted from life. While being successful in my businesses and having a great family was very important, my adventurous spirit took over. So I figured it was time to buy a good, well-trained horse like Eagle. That should make it easier to get in and out of that camp. But, then I needed a saddle, a horse trailer, and definitely a pack mule that would carry all my stuff. The guys told me that I'd also need a handgun for protection, perhaps even a rifle if I wanted to hunt with them. The guns would not only protect me, but could also save one of them if they were pounced upon by one of these hairy monsters. That was enough for me. I bought a hunting rifle, a .357 handgun, and naturally...a cowboy hat. Bill and I set up a target range on my rural acreage in Merced. After I successfully missed shooting any neighbors (none that I know of anyway), I finally began hitting the middle of the target.

When the snow melted in the high country, much of my business and social life took a backseat. Nothing was more exciting for me and Bill than to load our horses and mules and head out to our wilderness camp where something really big was lurking. And that unseen 'something' walked on two feet, vocalized with the amplitude of an 800-pound gorilla on steroids, and still remained an enigma.

It was the spring of 1972 and the high country snow was giving way to dry ground. My wife was not too thrilled about the whole Bigfoot/monster goings-on, but understood how eager I was to be a part of this unusual adventure. I had become proficient with my guns, liked eating venison, and was ready to join the others. Bill had bought a couple of well-seasoned pack mules, and I had a well-trained half-Arabian horse, JR, along with a young inexperienced mule.

A good, well-trained horse will usually do what his master wants but that's not necessarily true with young head-strong mules. They seem to consider issues before making their move. But, I thought I was ready and nothing could have stopped me from riding up that mountain with Bill.

Riding a horse was not just fun, but I could also see a lot more from high up in the saddle; for sure I'd have time to look for a hairy beast. Plus, I didn't smell as sweaty after getting to camp. For many domesticated animals this imposing trail is difficult to negotiate. It would also prove to be especially challenging for this new rider. Leading a young and vigorous pack mule was also new for me. My future of wrangling in and out of that mountainous area was to be filled with high-level adventure and packed with lots of backwoods education.

Because of the need for our animals to acclimate to the elevation, and also the time required making the trip into camp, we slept the first night at the trailhead. As previously mentioned, the first couple of miles are very steep with mostly switchbacks and lots of large boulders to negotiate. I was wrangling Rabbit, my semi-perverted, three-year-old mule. This mule would soon establish his personal boundaries and definitely not live up to his name. It's common knowledge that rabbits can hop, jump or leap. Rabbit was carrying a lot of our camping supplies on his back. He was also carrying all my stuff, including a new, top-of-the-line, portable stereo tape recorder. I don't think he liked any of it.

Author 1972

Halfway up the switchbacks there is a spot where the animals need to lunge onto a boulder in order to not get hung up on some exposed cedar roots. I figured I'd let JR have his nose and just hang on. He knew what to do and I was pretty sure he didn't want to fall. So I tied the rope, by which I was wrangling Rabbit, securely around my saddle horn, or so I thought. I grabbed JR's mane and kicked him, which wasn't the smartest thing I'd ever done. Rabbit held his ground when JR lunged. I guess he wanted to think about his part of that jump a little longer (or maybe he'd just been waiting for this chance to get even for all that stuff I put on his back). Rabbit dug in his hooves and with an unfamiliar little spin, JR and I went tumbling over the edge. Rabbit's lead rope conveniently came off JR's saddle horn.

As my life flashed before me, all I remember seeing was leather and horse hooves as we plummeted down this almost vertical embankment. I came out of the saddle but continued to roll on down with JR, stopping myself about halfway. I somehow escaped getting any broken bones, but make no mistake, it hurt. I was lying there stunned as I watched my horse continue to tumble on down. It seemed like slow-motion, until he finally crashed into a huge cedar tree. Heck, the lower switchback was only a few more feet away. The mountainside became really quiet then. As I looked down at JR lying there motionless, an awful thought ran through my mind. I may have to shoot the horse and carry the saddle. But, as I looked up at Rabbit it occurred to me, if I had to shoot my horse he was going to carry the saddle – a real John Wayne moment. I worked my way down to the very motionless JR, but saw he was still breathing. I thought surely he would have at least a broken leg, but somehow he, too, had escaped without serious injury.

To say the least JR was shaken, but with my help was able to get up. So I led him to the lower switchback, checked out his skinned-up hide and limped back up to meet with Bill. Eagle and the mules were calmly standing there, nibbling on whatever greenery they found appealing. I didn't even want to look at Rabbit. The saddle's rigging was badly torn, but thanks to some really strong nylon string and a leather punch that Bill convinced me to bring, I was able to patch it back together. After completing all the repairs, I gave Rabbit a dirty look, quietly mumbled a couple choice words, and while he wasn't paying attention, gave a quick jerk on his cinch. I took a deep breath, found my hat and got back on JR.

Up switchbacks: Front: Bill McDowell w/Eagle and mules.
Rear: Larry Johnson

What I was beginning to learn is how much better mule's survival instincts seem to be than what a horse has. Mules are really tough, rarely get into trouble and rarely get hurt, unlike a well-trained horse, which generally respects his master's command – especially when his master is wearing spurs.

The incident had taken too much time out of our day, and we needed to get moving. In a way I felt 'okay' because it didn't give Rabbit time to plot another "How do I get even with Ron?" episode. But this was just the beginning of a long and memorable relationship between Rabbit, JR and me.

My adventures over the years with Rabbit were educational and make a completely different, amusing, and perhaps entertaining story unto itself. More importantly, however, the year brought a truly memorable season with these big-footed visitors coming around our camp.

Author, JR and Rabbit

Author at camp after a bear rummaged

Chapter 5

Incidents and Other Sounds

Most of the events that took place in 1972 were hair-raising, but also brought me to the realization that these creatures are very observant and command respect for their reasoning ability. I also began to think that the guns might not be necessary for protection from Bigfoot. But we all continued to carry them anyway. It didn't seem to bother these big guys, and the firearms provided a definite sense of security. The guns strapped to our sides, coupled with the cowboy hats and pack mules, also allowed us to step back from our day jobs and become the adventurous Wild West outdoorsmen that we only got to see in the movies. But this adventure was unquestionably set apart from any I'd ever seen in a theater.

In our minds there were other good reasons to carry guns. In my home, and sometimes on my head, sits a fancy 10X Stetson cowboy hat with a hatband from a 52-inch rattlesnake who greeted Bill and me on the trail. And one never knows how a bear might react if surprised accidentally, or heaven forbid, if it was a sow with cubs. I've heard about men that came between a sow and her little ones and I was sure I didn't want to become a character in one of those stories.

Bear are plentiful in this region and, apparently, we had a family of Bigfoots coexisting with them. But to me these creatures were definitely becoming more than just another animal roaming the woods. Unlike bears, they were visiting us almost nightly and interacting with some very unusual vocalizations that were directed at us -- including a very unusual type of whistle.

Play Soundtrack (4)

After their sounds quit and we got into our sleeping bags, they would often return during the night's stillness. It was mostly still anyway. I won't mention names, but some of the guys snored, and getting to sleep 'first' meant you got some sleep that night. Between the vibrations of snoring, I heard the pine-needles crunching just outside our "hutchie" (a term coined by Louis for the shelter). The sound was like a two-legged elephant sneaking through the woods. There was heavy breathing,

27

coming from the same area just a few feet away.

Play Soundtrack (5)

I lay motionless, waiting for a flicker to break the moonlit cracks in the deadfall walls. Something – something disturbingly real – was causing my heart to race and my imagination to run wild. I should have been scared, but I wasn't – I just wanted see something, then maybe I'd be scared and could punch one of those snorers.

The shelter is made of deadfall logs leaning on cables which are strapped to a circle of trees. Its opening is questionably secured by one big vertical log. This log leans between two cedars and a rope holds it secure. After arriving in camp, we routinely untied the opening, removed the log door and put back together what the bears or "something" had tore apart. It was usual for some type of wilderness intruder to rip open a large hole in the top, enter, look around and ravage the place. Once, we were missing some Plaster of Paris, which we used for casting Bigfoot prints. We figured a bear took it and probably ate it. Assuming the bear didn't die, he surely had some trauma to deal with later... can you imagine? Now and then one of these unprincipled scavengers would break into our ringed barrels, which were cabled to the trees outside, and eat anything it could get in its mouth. We'd later find coils of foil in bear feces strung out over the mountainside – defecation with a silver lining, what an amazing digestive system.

After organizing the shelter, our custom was to get our sleeping area arranged for the night. While it was still daylight, we set up our recorders, anticipating that these hairy forest dwellers would come around that night and sound off. Generally, I placed my microphone somewhere in the crevice of the shelter's walls and kept my recorder switch by my sleeping bag. To keep our recorders' activation noise as quiet as possible, most of us rigged up a quiet mercury switch that would start the recording. All we had to do was turn the switch over and our recorders would silently begin recording.

One evening Warren and I were inside the shelter when these creatures started their rapid chattering. One of them sounded like he was very close. Frustrated by our non-working tricks of camera traps and food traps, we pondered how to get a look at one – and a picture of one, too. We decided to not take our guns with us, so we were armed with only our cameras. With our sock-hats on, we darted out through the opening, thinking we'd see it run away. With the bright moonlight working in our favor, we looked in the direction we thought the chatter had been coming from. But nothing ran away...nothing moved...no sound...nothing! We could have heard a pin drop in that forest.

We were about 15 feet apart as we began slowly creeping up the ridge. My eyes were opened as wide as they could get and I wasn't about to blink. Surely this creature had to be behind one of those giant cedars. After walking about 30 feet and at exactly the same time, we both froze in our tracks, unable to move forward. We were just a few feet from a huge cedar when we looked at each other. "I don't know about you, but I can't go any farther – we need to go back," Warren said. I agreed. This paralyzing effect was not explainable, and it wasn't fear. It may sound crazy, but it seemed we were being blocked by a force field, like in the old Star Trek episodes.

Several years later I brought this up to a scientist who believed in the possibility of the Bigfoot phenomenon. He said that feelings and science don't go together. I said that I didn't think the event was a feeling. We were literally unable to move forward and I suggested that perhaps science should think on this. Given the way it happened (to both of us at the same time), I really didn't think the sensation was self-induced. He suggested the possibility of pheromones, or maybe infrasound.

Of course, nowadays, infrasound (sound below the limit of human hearing) is widely accepted as a factor that can affect human emotions. It can even make the hair stand up on the back of the neck – that was familiar to me. At one time or another all the hunters at the Sierra camp have experienced a type of sensation that may have been the result of infrasound. The lower frequency of infrasound was used in World War II by Nazi propaganda engineers to stir up anger in large crowds that gathered to hear Hitler. Large animals such as elephants, giraffes and whales use infrasound to communicate and find others of their species over long distances. Tigers hunt using infrasound and can temporarily paralyze their prey (Fauna Communications Research Institute). But I don't think the sensation that Warren and I experienced was from a tiger or an elephant, and whales definitely don't hang out in the mountains.

JR & Author w/ rattlesnake hatband, 1976

Does Bigfoot use infrasound? Many times, as I lay in my sleeping bag listening to their huge bipedal footsteps and their heavy breathing, I've asked myself, "Why can't I jump up – and run out of the shelter and snap a picture?" I don't know what was affecting me (or how), but something kept me there...something with the same paralyzing effect. It was not fear and I still wonder how it was caused.

There were several events that caused me to think we might be in the Twilight Zone. We didn't take alcohol to camp and the only smoke that could have got into our lungs would have been from the stove fire. On occasions, however, always during the day, we heard what sounded like a huge tuning fork. None of us knew what to make of that sound but it reminded me of someone trying to tune a piano for someone that was really hard of hearing. We never did see anything that may have been responsible for those sounds, nor have I ever been told of anyone outside of our group claiming to have heard that type of sound. And to be clear, we never saw a spaceship.

There was also another very unusual type of sound we experienced one night. After bedding down, we heard crashing, rowdy metallic sounds. It sounded like our ringed barrels, where we stored our food, were rolling down towards the creek. These barrels were bound to the trees with cables and to rip them from those trees would have demanded a bulldozer. But when we gazed out of the shelter, we noticed that they had not been moved – not even a little...nothing had been disturbed. And we didn't see anything around that could have caused those sounds.

Bill McDowell and Author at Camp

A mysterious unexplained 'clicking' sound happened when Bill, Louis and I were in camp. After we bedded down, we heard this type of sound coming from our stove area – no dancers with castanets were there either. As we lay quietly in our sleeping bags, listening, the sound came closer. Soon these clicking sounds were just outside our doorway – we didn't see any shadows and it wasn't a cricket. Then without notice, the clicking was inside the shelter – the log door was firmly in place. We all three immediately turned on our flashlights but nothing was there. When we turned off our lights, the sound would start up again. We'd shine our lights and the sound would stop again.

We discussed what type of critter could be doing that and it was then we decided to leave our lights off and see what happened. As we lay motionless in our sleeping bags, the clicking sound began slowly making its way up between Louis and me. We talked to each other as it moved closer, and decided that when it got within grabbing range we would shine our lights at the same time – what guts, huh? Our talking didn't seem to deter the sound. As it got within inches of us, we shined our lights – but nothing was there. After that the clicking stopped.

To elevate this mystery, the same clicking sound was with me a week later during the day at my valley ranch while I was irrigating. Daytime isn't quite as spooky in the valley and I didn't see any shadows, but it was still unexplainable. The sound actually followed me. At first I thought it may have been something on me, perhaps a rock dangling from my boot, or maybe a musical cricket having fun. But none of those proved out. Several years later I asked Bill if he'd ever had anything unusual take place outside of our camp. Without telling him of my irrigating experience, he told me that within a week or so after that clicking experience at camp, he'd had the exact same sound following him while he was in his pasture. What could make this type of sound show up a week later, at an elevation 8000 feet lower? And what connection could it have with our camp... or us?

Chapter 6

Tricks & Traps

Except for the clicking sound at my ranch, all of those mysterious sounds seemed to be associated with the presence of Bigfoot. As much as possible we would schedule our trips when the weather was supposed to be good and when the moon was in our favor. However, it became apparent that while we were in their territory, moon or no moon, rain or no rain, any interaction would be on their terms.

These creatures were able to stay one step ahead of every trick we tried to obtain a picture. We all thought that some good pictures shouldn't be too hard to get. After all, these giants were getting fairly bold around us. During the remaining months of 1971, and also during 1972, our carefully engineered camera traps only produced broken cameras andobviously no pictures of whatever was making those sounds.

To capture a picture, we considered several ideas. During the day, when five of us were in camp, Warren had a brainstorm. We draped a small semi-transparent camouflage net over a rotted-out hollow stump which was about 30 feet from the shelter's opening. It was going to be another brisk and still night. Warren's plan was to hide inside that stump. But we needed to figure out a diversion. Evening came and Bigfoot did, too. He was loud and rowdy, but this time we had a plan. We all darted from inside the shelter and spread out in different directions while Warren quickly slipped inside that stump and threw the net over him. As he squatted silently at his post with his camera ready, the rest of us retreated back inside. I guess Warren's plan was to either throw the net aside and snap the picture or just get a fuzzy picture through that net. We hadn't thought past that to consider the effect the flash might have on Bigfoot. 5 minutes passed, then 15, then 30, but nothing was happening. Finally, Warren's hands were about to freeze to the camera, so he gave it up and came back into the shelter. In less than a minute Bigfoot was sounding off again.

Our plan came with good forethought, I thought it was executed with military precision, and it went quite well. Except we didn't get a picture, nor did Warren see anything. This incident, coupled with our other efforts to get a better look, was very frustrating. How could an animal living in the forest be so tuned in to our human connivings?

We lost three cameras before we figured out that they were probably figuring us out. One method we tried was to mount the camera to a tree (about 6 feet high) and rig up a black thread between the trees that would trigger the camera. It seemed like a foolproof plan. After all, they'd been coming in from that same direction to get the food. These traps never had a successful outcome and our camera supply was dwindling. To say nothing about the film that got exposed when the camera was batted off the tree. Al Berry tried a camera with infrared film and infrared flashbulbs. That, too, was unsuccessful. I guess they just didn't want their picture taken. Shy perhaps or maybe just having a bad hair day. Warren and Al actually bought an expensive starlight scope, hoping for a look at one of these big guys. We all carried a camera at all times, just in case we got lucky during the day.

We were always on the lookout for these giants, especially during hunting season. It seemed they were more active during this time. Maybe they were interested in our hunting methods, or perhaps they enjoyed the deer remains. Or, because of hunting season, maybe they felt safe around our area. Rarely were there any other hunters within miles of our camp. At the first sign of light, with our cameras and rifles, we'd leave the horses and mules tied up and go hunting on foot. We stealthily walked through the woods and, after a while, separated a couple of hundred yards apart. Moving slowly through the forest, we made as little noise as possible. In this manner everyone could generally get within range of a buck, and we thought this might also allow us to sneak within camera range of a Bigfoot, perhaps catching one of them eyeballing one of the other hunters in our group.

After the kill – and there was always a kill – the shooter would gut the deer and take the heart and liver out so they could be prepared for the evening meal. We would leave the carcass to be picked up later with the horses and mules (except for Rabbit, of course; he refused to carry a dead deer). Around noon, at a pre-arranged place, we would meet for lunch and talk about the hunt, who had gotten a deer and who needed to keep hunting. Depending on how many deer needed to be picked up, Bill and I would continue to hunt or head back and saddle up. Most of the time we would head back to camp, get the animals and make a sweep to pick up the deer.

Bear would ravage the deer if we left them in the forest overnight, so often it would be a challenge to beat the fading daylight. Sometimes Bill and I would need to make more than one trip to pick up all the deer. More than once, when we arrived back in camp to get our horses, we found big five-toed footprints around them. Ah, if our animals could have only talked – or operated a camera!

After our return to camp, we'd hang the deer on a cable behind the shelter where later they would be skinned. Sometimes, after a visit from our giant friends, the next morning we would notice huge footprints under the deer. Figuring they were curious about the skinned deer, late one afternoon, Larry, Warren's son, and I smoothed out an area under the deer – hoping to obtain a really clear print. We then joined the others around the stove for the usual feast of fresh liver and heart. After we gorged ourselves for close to an hour, it was dark.

Larry and I took our flashlights to check out the backside of the shelter again. The deer had been moved and there were three big foot impressions on the ground. The shelter is about 8 feet high, and the stove is about 50 feet from where we hung the deer. Although I figured these creatures had been observing us, this real-time spy-job really brought that awareness to the forefront of my mind... it was a bit unsettling.

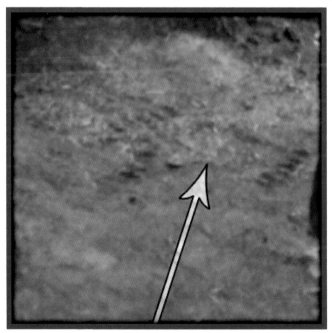

Deer carcass w/three giant foot impressions

On another occasion we had stew for dinner and Jell-O for dessert (we just boiled the water, mixed in the Jell-O and set it in the snow for a while). We'd left the large serving spoon in the leftover stew, and the remainder of the Jell-O was a few feet away. Just after we went into our shelter, we heard Bigfoot's menacing sounds coming from our stove area. After about 30 minutes these sounds ended. The next morning we noticed all the stew was gone, which could be expected, but the shocker was the large serving spoon was in the now-empty Jell-O pan.

Bill McDowell w/mules and deer carcass

Al Berry's boot w/cast

Chapter 7

Intelligent Reasoning, Gifts & Kids

B esides the suggestion of mimicking our eating habits, other interesting events took place that caused our heads to turn. When preparing a stove fire, we gathered pinecones and small twigs for kindling. We used an old rusted-out wash pan to gather the pinecones from nearby trees. Once, after the morning's fire, all the pinecones had been used. We left for a hike and after a few hours we returned. The wash pan was full of pinecones. I believe this 'gifting' was just another way for them to interact with us.

With friendly gestures of offering and their obvious endeavors to interact, and after consideration, Bill and I thought our children would be safe at this camp. They were old enough to enjoy this pristine wilderness and should be exposed to its wonderful, but sometimes challenging, elements.

But what would Bigfoot think? Neither Bill nor I believed we would overreact if our children panicked due to a sighting and the children had heard our sound recordings many times. But Bigfoot may have known more about how we would react than us. If a child screamed out of fear or accidently wandered off, it would be very concerning to us, and our reaction could compromise Bigfoot's desire to maintain an open line of welcomed communication with the group. While our kids were in camp, there was never any Bigfoot interaction.

Bill brought his son Dale, and I brought my daughter Rhonda. On the second day, Bill asked Dale if he would like to experience the joy of digging a fresh pit for our trash. Bill and I napped while Rhonda watched Dale dig the hole. This left a fresh mound of dirt, and Dale should have been proud of his accomplishment.

Dale McDowell

Bill McDowell

This loose mound of dirt turned into a convenient pile for Bigfoot a week later when Warren, Bill and I returned to camp. We found some leftover tainted lunch meat in our supply barrel and decided to leave it out for these creatures. That night we also inadvertently left the lid off a jar of hot peppers. Bigfoot had been chattering around our stove area that night, and the next morning the pepper jar was empty. Most surprising to us, beneath a huge handprint in the fresh mound of dirt from Dale's pit, was the tainted lunch meat – it had been buried.

Although these giants had been taking our leftover cooked food, we still considered their diet to be like that of a bear, which will eat almost anything. But they never took our hanging deer, perhaps out of respect for our hunt, or maybe they didn't want to draw that kind of attention. Bad lunch meat was obviously not agreeable, and I can only guess what they thought about those hot peppers.

In spite of our well intentioned, but ill received offering of bad meat, Bigfoot continued to interact and didn't seem to hold any grudges. About 100 feet up an incline behind our shelter is a large boulder outcrop – a good spot for an 8-foot-tall creature to stealthily observe our camp. The sky was clear, the moon was bright again, and the forest was dead silent. Suddenly we heard Bigfoot sounds coming from behind those rocks and this time, out of frustration to see one, we decided to be the aggressors... stir up some action, so to speak. Slowly, Louis, Al and I walked up the incline and gradually moved to a sandy clearing behind those boulders. While standing there, I gave out a whistle. Immediately I received a return whistle from the wooded area about 50 feet away. This was my first direct interaction with them and an exciting 'wow' for all three of us. It wasn't until afterwards that Al realized none of us had our side arms – another 'wow'. Our must-have, gun-totin' security blanket had been foiled, and we didn't even realize it at the time.

Normally, we didn't go outside the shelter without our handguns. We still didn't know what we were dealing with, but whatever they were, we thought they were very unique, and our encounters were quite the novelty. Often they seemed to be toying with us and may have found our presence in their forest interesting. Bit by bit, I think they were beginning to trust that we would not shoot at them. And bit by bit, we continued moving to the conclusion that they were not going to harm us. I think it would have been easy for them to just hurl a rock, and we would have been in our eternal resting place.

Larry Johnson had told us that rocks the size of softballs were being thrown over his head while he was taking an imposing route to camp that is rarely used. They were hitting a tree about 10 feet away and he thought they were definitely intended to get his attention. Over the years there have been many reports of these creatures throwing rocks but never has anyone claimed that they were hit. When they throw rocks, I think it might be to deter an intruder and maybe keep that person away from a young Bigfoot. The small voice heard around our camp a few times, which I recorded in the 70s, was probably an adolescent. Oh, by the way, bears don't throw rocks – we were dealing with something that has an opposable thumb.

Al Berry and I responded to a report from some men in Plumas County in northern California. They claimed that these creatures were harassing them – even claimed a sighting. We went deep into the mountains with them to an abandoned mining camp. That night while we were chatting around the fire, a rock was thrown past us and struck a tree nearby. That rock had to have been catapulted by something with great strength. It zipped by us with the speed of an arrow. We found the grapefruit-sized rock the next morning at the base of the tree and saw where the bark was missing high on the tree. I believe that like people and other animals, these creatures have different personalities. Some are easily angered, some will "toy" with humans, and some will interact. Al was recording the conversation of these men and actually captured the sound of that rock whizzing by.

Chapter 8

Al Berry

Al served as an officer in Vietnam and had seen plenty of action, but this type of action that Peter Byrne asked him to investigate was obviously different. Al was the newest addition to this small group of hunters, but he didn't hunt. To get to camp, Al had to travel a much longer distance, so he wasn't able to get there as often as the rest of us. His attitude around camp seemed to be completely different than ours. While we hiked and hunted, he stayed at camp, often taking notes, documenting everything. Our story and these sounds seemed difficult for Al to accept and his actions gave me the impression that he thought one of us may have just been having fun. He desperately wanted to determine the source of these sounds.

Years later, Al told me that he searched our packs while we were day-hiking. It seemed like his main reason for being there was to uncover a hoax. I guess that's typical of what investigators do with a story like this. But, as previously noted, the camp is hard to get to, over some rough, imposing country, and at this time we didn't understand how he could doubt what we perceived as reality. From our experiences with these creatures, having not been harmed, we surmised that we were fairly safe. I think our nonchalant demeanor may have seemed strange to Al and I'm not sure he understood that. Bill, a hard worker, could actually fall asleep while these noises were being made, but Al stayed alert, was doing a job and desperately wanted to get to the bottom of this.

In 1972, he brought in a small top-of-the-line Sony cassette tape recorder. It was surpassed only by my Sony TC-153SD recorder. My recorder was the best portable stereo cassette money could buy, and I recorded more quality vocalizations than anyone. Unfortunately, in 1976, my recorder and all my original tapes were consumed in a house fire. But, fortunately, some of my sounds were copied to others in the group. However, Al's recordings from his 1972 trip turned out great and were later to be used for the professional analysis that he had done.

Play Soundtrack (6)

In 1976, Al decided to tell his story and co-authored the Bantam Book, *Bigfoot* with Ann Slate. In the first three chapters of that book he tells of the unique Sierra adventure and his efforts to flush out the fun-maker. Al has often told me that he thinks the story would actually be better if it was a hoax – how could anyone have pulled this off?

It would be years before my relationship with Al would become solidified with understanding and respect. I think he finally understood the issue of our complacency and I finally understood his professional approach to this mystery. Eventually, he and I became entwined, speaking at symposiums and conferences, analyzing data from others, and often travelled far-away to go on an expedition together.

In the summer of 1973, Al decided to spend several weeks at the camp with his brother. Bill and I took supplies to them with our horses and mules. There were no Bigfoot vocalizations at all. During one night in June, Al heard the rather brisk bipedal walk of a single creature during the night. The next morning he cast its 14-inch track. That was all he noted during the whole summer, and it was probably a bit concerning. All of us wondered if our Bigfoot interaction might be over.

This lack of activity during 1973 was cause for several conversations that winter, and actually a deeper desire to learn more about these creatures. We had begun to feel a kindred-type spirit with them and really wanted the adventure to continue.

Al Berry and Author at camp

Al Berry and Author

We started to refer to them collectively as "Biggie." One could assume that someone (could be one of us) might obtain enough evidence to convince science of Biggie's existence. Mainstream science demands undisputable proof, like a body. Hunting them would surely stop the welcomed rapport we felt we had built, and our thoughts were definitely not in that direction. It seemed wrong, somehow, to shoot something just for a scientific discovery. It's also wrong, in my opinion, to shoot something because it is not understood.

The topic of not killing one has been a focal point at conferences where Al and I have spoken. We didn't consider shooting one an option, unless of course we felt threatened. Perhaps, somehow Biggie knew this.

Al Berry and Author speaking at a conference (2005)

Chapter 9

1974 Interaction

During 1974, getting time away from work was difficult for some of the guys. So on three occasions I actually went to the Sierra camp alone. I have to say that on those quiet nights, I would have liked it better if someone was there to look over my shoulder. Plainly speaking, it's spooky being there alone. I might add that going to camp by myself was also a way for me to face the unknown, a possible measure of my nerve. I was 32 years old, impulsive and thought I was indestructible.

In retrospect, going alone was probably a bonehead, stupid thing to do. Besides not knowing for sure exactly the type creature we had been dealing with in this remote area of the wilderness, if I broke a leg, became caught in really bad weather, or anything terrible happened, I may never be found – and could turn into bear food. Notwithstanding accidents, at that time I thought it was okay because none of us had been attacked, carried away in our sleeping bag, or harmed in any way.

Although there were no vocalizations during the previous year, I still hoped that Biggie was around and would interact. However, due to the lack of corroboration by someone else, confirmation of possible Biggie activity would have been arguable. When alone, imagination can run rampant; was that sound or that flicker real, or the product of my imagination? Could it have been a restless mountain lion, maybe a bear, or was it Biggie? When by myself, my .357 magnum handgun was on my side and fully loaded at all times. Not that I'm afraid of the dark, but I went inside the shelter before it got that way. The log door was tied as tight as I could get it, and only my eyes and ears were poking out of the sleeping bag. Every sound emanating from the forest seemed amplified and I thought daylight would never come. These nights felt like the longest nights I'd ever experienced at our camp.

My summer's nonproductive alone trips faded into September's hunting season with Bill. Were our Bigfoot experiences over? The sheer anticipation of more interaction was still an issue taking up a large space in my brain. But unbeknownst to us, we were about to have an unsurpassed interactive experience with these giants of the Sierras.

At the first sign of daybreak Bill and I began transporting our horses and mules from the valley to the trailhead. It was two days before hunting season and we needed to take fresh supplies to ready the camp. After we arrived we saddled the horses, packed the mules, and hurried up the trail trying to make camp before dark.

About ¼ mile up the trail, our horses and mules were startled by something. We thought little of it, probably a deer or bear milling around. However, about an hour later, as the switchbacks opened up to a sandy area, my attention began to be more focused on animal trail-sign, rather than the drop-offs and rattle snakes. We all prided ourselves on seeing what animals had been using the trail, then we would try to assess how old the sign might be.

It was a relief to not have to grab JR's mane for support in those steep spots of the trail, or be overly concerned about Rabbit showing his individuality. I was in the lead position when I noticed a fresh five-toed footprint perpendicular to the trail. That was a "show-stopper." My adrenaline rushed, my eyes must have gotten bigger and I immediately got off my horse and called Bill. Our jaws dropped as we silently gazed at this 22-inch print. I took a picture, and then I stuck my boot next to it and snapped another. I placed my watch next to it and took another. We didn't have the time, nor did we have any casting material or water nearby, to make a cast and wait for it to dry. Our horses and mules would have obliterated the print, but I smeared it out anyway. In a day or two other hunters could be using this part of the trail, and I wanted to make sure the print didn't draw any unnecessary attention.

We had little doubt that our giant friends were with us again, and it was exciting. I hadn't noticed any human tracks on the trail and very few animal signs. We discussed the location of the track and noted that it was right at the top of a ravine that led down to where our animals were startled earlier. It seems these creatures go out of their way to not leave tracks or any evidence of their presence, and this footprint appeared too obvious. I think it may have been intentionally left for us to see.

Bill and I pressed the animals without stopping. The horses and mules were in great shape and our desire to get into camp before dark was increasing by the moment. We felt fairly confident that Biggie had no intention of harming us, but it's still not fun trying to find our camp after dark, especially knowing something still unidentified, very big, and obviously much stronger than us could jump out from behind those trees at anytime and yell "Boo". Plus, it can get confusing on the way in after dark. However, the animals knew where they were going and have much better night vision than we do. With daylight fading this became reassuring. I just needed to watch out for those low-hanging tree limbs.

We arrived at dusk. The animals were beat and so were we. By 1974 Bill and I had made a lot of pack trips and we had become well-coordinated. We knew what needed to be done and each of us could do it without saying much. Daylight was vanishing. The huge cedar trees shadowed the camp area and the moon was just beginning to peek over the mountain's ridge line. We had a lot to do. Immediately I gathered firewood and pinecones for a fire. Bill unloaded our supplies and began to take care of the animals. After I got water from the spring and started a fire, we began to settle in and relax. I had just begun heating up a can of stew, when we heard a large limb break.

When these creatures break a limb, it's not like hearing a large animal step on a limb. The sound is huge, sharp and has definition.

Play Soundtrack (7)

It was them, or at least one of them. I think that's what they do to get attention and observe the response. Bill and I looked at each other, calmly reached in our saddlebags, got our recorders, smiled at each other, and kept doing what we were doing.

Usually the creatures will come in closer if they think they're being ignored. It wasn't but a moment later that we heard rocks begin to pop together and a large limb being rhythmically banged against a boulder.

Play Soundtrack (8)

I don't believe those types of sounds were meant for us, but rather they may be signaling to another family member. Or, who knows? It could be that they just like to play with limbs and rocks. They have really good rhythm.

Play Soundtrack (9)

The sounds began from about 60 yards away, across the creek, and down from our shelter, close to a large rock outcrop. We could see those rocks, and the sounds echoed very clearly on this crisp moonlit evening. Our horses and mules didn't seem bothered by the noises, but that wasn't unusual. Normally, they're motionless with their ears pointed toward the sounds. After a few minutes of rock-popping and limb-breaking, the creatures began to whoop back and forth. The whoops had different intonations and different sequences, and came from different directions. We hadn't heard whoops like this before. Possibly another way they have of signaling each other.

Play Soundtrack (10)

Suddenly the pace changed, and the real excitement began when one of the creatures actually said something. It seemed to be directed at us. It sounded like some form of language, having organization or meaning of some type. We continued to eat and tried to pay little attention to the sounds. Overreacting to their displays had not proven effective in the past, as they seem to want to be in charge. These vocalizations, however, prompted a response from me. I tried to mimic the sound and immediately received a reply that contained an array of primitive-sounding vocalizations.

Play Soundtrack (11)

Okay, what now? Were these things trying to talk to us? Seems like it, but what were they saying? My other thought was, "What did I say back to trigger such a response?" It was almost like they thought it was humorous.

Play Soundtrack (12)

With this type of boldness being displayed, we wondered if they were finally going to let us see them. Other brief sightings around camp had been by sheer luck. If these things would just let us have a look at them tonight, intentionally, that would really step this chronicle up a notch. We'd never had them be this forward with their vocalizations, especially while we were still outside our shelter. And this time, for some unknown reason, their noises seemed friendly, more meaningful, and not as aggressive-sounding as in the past.

During the vocal exchange, I heard what sounded like a question. It was definitely directed at me. "Aush trosh trio?" I paused, and again... "Aush trosh trio?" Okay, I'll answer! But, again, how should I respond?

Play Soundtrack (13)

As best I could, I mimicked the sound and immediately received what I thought was another query. "Appala?"…"Appala?" Again I tried as best I could to mimic that sound.

Play Soundtrack (14)

I was curious as to what was being asked and what my response might have meant to them. Between instances of vocalizing in our direction, it sounded like they were discussing, or perhaps arguing, among themselves.

At one point I heard a large voice and a small voice. It sounded confrontational, like a mother scolding her child. Could there be a young, bold Bigfoot being a little disobedient?

Play Soundtrack (15)

If my assessment was correct, it suggested that there were at least three and one was a child. In the spring of 1972, we found a small 7-inch footprint in the snow next to an 18-inch print and at that time we figured we were dealing with a family of these creatures. On another occasion during the day, after following some tracks away from camp, Larry, Warren and Louis claimed to have heard what sounded like an adolescent being scolded by an adult. They said the sounds came from a heavily wooded area about 30 yards away from where they were.

Big, little, male or female, on this night these creatures were definitely bolder than ever before. Suddenly Bill jerked with excitement and whispered, "There's one, did ya see it?"

Play Soundtrack (16)

Prior to this evening neither Bill nor I had ever even had a glimpse of one, but this evening was to be different. Although the night obscured the details of these huge, shadowy figures, before it was over both Bill and I would have brief sightings of what was making these noises – it had been a long time coming for me.

Sierra Camp Corral Area: Rabbit showing his individuality

Then it was my turn to get a glimpse. It may have been a creature trying to prompt a response from us, or perhaps one was just having fun, but it was playing with our makeshift toilet. About 50 feet from our stove, inside a small semi-circle of trees, we'd dug a hole, laid small logs around that hole, packed in a toilet seat and *voila*, our throne. At one point we heard the lid of that seat bang a couple times, and it was then we discussed shining a light.

Play Soundtrack (17)

Although there were a few trees between us and the toilet seat, we might have had a pretty good look had we shined a light. But from previous encounters with these creatures, we found that shining a flashlight in their direction would drive them off.

Play Soundtrack (18)

They are extremely stealthy, and like many nocturnal animals, they shy away from white light. At this elevation, on bright moonlit nights, the visibility is very good. When we did need a light to eat by, we'd generally use a kerosene lantern, which gives an amber glow.

Only a few moments after the toilet lid banged I saw a large, dark figure bolting through the moonlit trees with the speed of a running horse. Biggie was leaving that area and headed toward where the other sounds were coming from. It was running fast, very fast, but smooth, without any bouncing. I had to wonder how it was able to do that without tripping or stumbling on something. But like a horse, they probably have much larger eyes than we do and can see those limbs and rocks better than us. And, being completely at home in this wilderness, running fast like that is probably an everyday happening for them.

Then came another sound followed by different types of whoops. Again, I mimicked with my own whoops and I think these creatures were actually trying to have fun with me. I was certainly having fun with them.

Play Soundtrack (19)

Then we heard a long, drawn-out, very unusual cry coming from another direction – a sound so inhuman-like it shocked me. In no way could I mimic that sound. It would later be dubbed as "The Samurai Chatter."

Play Soundtrack (20)

It's been suggested that the sound was not directed at us but meant for one of the other creatures – perhaps a male with concerns about his family getting too close to us humans.

Another interactive sequence between one of the creatures and me began. I had no idea what was being said, but I carried on with my mimicking gibberish anyway.

Play Soundtrack (21)

We had vocal interaction back and forth for over an hour and the connection we were making was not only exciting but invaluable. Bill needed to turn his cassette tape over. I shined my small flashlight so that he could see better. The reflection of the light coming from the lid of his recorder flickered into the trees and like a switch, the vocalizations stopped - Damn, it didn't take much.

We stayed by our stove fire a bit longer but then grabbed our rifles, saddlebags, and recorders and went inside the shelter. We hoped they would start up again. As a rule we would lie quietly in our sleeping bags and listen for Biggie to make a noise. On previous occasions one of the sounds that announced their presence was a blowing sound, like a horse or mule after a difficult climb. This suggested to me that they had made a demanding hike to get to our camp. Or they could have been mimicking our animals. But on this night in 1974, I think they were in camp before we were, and probably had plenty of time to organize their reception party. However, our Biggie interaction was over for the night.

The next morning I peered out of the shelter and noticed Bill's dust cover from his rifle's scope. It was lying to the right of our opening on the edge of a Biggie footprint, but it was not smashed down. The round plastic cover had come off the night before as we went inside. That confirmed to me that Biggie had been there prior to our arrival.

However, the real sobering moment was about to come. To prevent leaks, every year or so the shelter would need to be re-roofed. We would remove the top layer of deadfall, roll out a fresh layer of plastic, put the deadfall back and cover it with fresh alder from the nearby spring. Earlier, in June we 'd done just that, but by now the fresh alder was dry. However, on this sunny morning of 1974 we noticed two fresh, green alder branches lying on top of the shelter with our dried ones from the summer. We located where these fresh, green, 1½-inch branches had been twisted off from the nearby spring. Whatever twisted off those branches would have to be much stronger than any human I know. This also suggested a creature with an opposable thumb, eliminating the probability that a bear would have done this (bears are not usually that accommodating anyway).

Author after re-roofing the shelter (1974)

For Bill and me, the twisted-off alders were a solid, rock-hard, jaw dropping, absolute head-turning confirmation of our earlier assessment. When we combined all the events from this trip – our animals being spooked shortly after we started up the trail, the obvious footprint we found on the trail, the footprint with Bill's dust cover leaning on it, and the welcome gift of fresh alder limbs on our shelter – we were certain that they recognized us early on and obviously knew where we were going. There was nobody at the trailhead and nobody had recently been on the trail. This suggests that these giants were just as happy about our coming to camp as we were to have them around again.

That afternoon Warren, Louis and Larry arrived in camp for the deer hunt, which was to begin the next morning. They asked about any Biggie activity, and we eagerly shared the prior evening's events. Would our big friends come around again? I was excited and was anticipating the arrival of dusk. For the most part, these creatures had previously responded to Warren's voice. He thought it might be less confusing if just one person spoke out to Biggie. However, when Warren wasn't in camp, I was the one who usually tried to interact with them. With Warren here now, and with what happened the night before, we joked that maybe they'd come in and join us for 'a spot of tea' or maybe give us a ride through the woods on their shoulders – wouldn't that be fun?

It was getting dark. We were all sitting around the stove eating and talking when, sure enough, Biggie started up with the whoops and the breaking of limbs. Since these encounters began three years earlier, we had eagerly waited for a time like this to evolve. No intimidating screams, horrific yells or stealthy crunching over the pine needles. Just a friendly "Hello, how are ya?" type sound. However, the tension seemed to get to Louis. He jumped up, grabbed his rifle and his flashlight, then rushed out toward the sounds saying; "I'm gonna find out what these things are all about, once and for all!" That immediately stopped all activity for the remainder of this trip.

Of course we understood Louis's frustration. We were all getting frustrated at the elusiveness of Biggie. But this act was a definite setback. No matter how much we tried our tricks to expose them, we seemed to be two notes behind the music. Often it seemed like a cat-and-mouse game to me. But I had to wonder, "Who was the cat and who was the mouse?"

Chapter 10

Bear Bones

Although we continued trekking to our camp and setting our traps, it wasn't until two years later that Biggie would again sound off. It was midnight in the summer of 1976 when Bill and I were awakened by a sound coming from the ridge behind our shelter. At the same time we heard something rummaging around our stove area. Except for the initial encounter that Warren and Louis had, this aggressive-type behavior had not been associated with Biggie. But if it was Biggie, he could have whatever he wanted – within reason of course.

The horses and mules were pawing and very restless, unlike the motionless persona they exhibited in the past when Biggie was around. We then heard our packs being ripped. These canvas packs had seen a lot of good times on top of a few good mules. They had served us well and we had become very protective of them. Just as important, however, they still contained some of our food. The ripping sound and the suggestion of what was happening to our supplies were becoming unacceptable. We felt a genuine need to shine a flashlight and take a gander at what was causing this fracas.

We looked out the shelter's opening only to see a black bear having his way with our stuff. We hurried out to chase him off. He went out about 30 yards and then began to circle the camp. As soon as we returned to the shelter, he was Johnny-on-the-spot back eating our food again. We got our guns ready, just in case. We ran out again, the bear left again, circled again and returned again. We came out of the shelter for the third time but this time the bear didn't go very far, only about 20 feet – I guess he decided he wanted the rest of our Red Delicious apples. And he must have realized too that he was much bigger than these little guys trying to run him off. He turned and stood up on two legs. That's when he looked really big. The bear gazed at us for a moment, probably considering how hungry he was and perhaps balancing his odds. But, as we stood there in our underwear, freezing and yelling and jumping up and down, he went down on all fours and charged at us. Bill instinctively shot the bear within just a few feet of us. The forest then became deadly quiet. I don't want to be redundant, but I mean deadly quiet. This type of behavior had never happened around camp before and it was extremely rare for a black bear in the Sierras to be that aggressive.

The next morning Bill skinned and butchered the bear. We dug a deep-pit barbeque and that evening we began eating that bear. Or, to be nice, began the recycling process of those apples. Unlike a greasy bear that feasts from garbage dumps, these high-country bears obviously satisfied their hunger with good wholesome mountain grub (except for the occasional stuff we humans bring in, like foil, Plaster of Paris, etc.). The bear was successfully transformed from one who eats our food to one who was our food.

Killing the bear (and perhaps eating it) seemed to mark the end of our close-in connection with Bigfoot. Only distant chatter and occasional wood knocking was to be heard for the next few years. Perhaps the trusting relationship we thought we had had now been compromised.

Bear rummaging stove area

*Right: Dale McDowell
after a bear rummaged camp.*

58

Chapter 11

Snapshot of the 70's

My take-away from 1971 is that the beginning vocalizations sounded very antagonistic, possibly territorial, like they wanted us to leave. Perhaps still a bit angry about being burned by the tea-pot water. Their rapid-fire vocal displays sounded ape-like and at times much like chest-beating. We also heard what sounded like teeth popping and the smacking of lips – maybe a bit challenged while trying to get down the peanut butter we left out.

Play Soundtrack (22)

In 1972 the sounds were still very aggressive, but also somewhat curious, like they were coming to terms with us being there. During that year Bill and I made a lot of pack trips into the camp, and also explored several other areas in the general region. We had numerous encounters, and we hadn't shot at them or panicked during their displays. Our non-threatening presence coupled with our cheerful attitude might have been appealing. I think they felt more secure with us and became bolder as summer passed and hunting season began. Perhaps they considered this group of men the ones with whom they could safely interact – but why? What was the point of their interactions?

The year of 1973 brought little activity. We don't know why. Al Berry was in camp most of the summer. He was also there for a different reason than the rest of us. Not to relax, not to hunt, but to seriously investigate this phenomenon. They may have sensed that difference between him and the hunters and had their guard up. He also had his brother with him most of the time and he was a new face. Perhaps they are more sensitive to our investigation methods than we realized. It's also a possibility that the Bigfoot family we dealt with the previous year had left. At one time in 1972 we noticed seven different-size prints around camp, which suggested two different families were present for a short period.

In 1974 they demonstrated a different sound, unlike any we'd previously heard, and a definite desire to vocally interact. The vocalizations these creatures made seemed like an concerted effort to slow down their rapid garble to what they may have considered something recognizable to us.

During 1975 we didn't make very many trips to camp, and the trips we did make were void of any noticeable activity from Biggie.

In 1976 was when we had to shoot the bear, and in afterthought, I've wondered if Biggie became a bit wary of our actions. This bear just wanted to eat and went for the food. We were the intruders, we left out the apples, and this was the bear's territory. We probably shouldn't have left our food so exposed.

The remainder of the 70's, and most of the 80's, only gave us occasional footprints to look at and infrequent, distant Biggie chatter. This was an indication that they were still around. Once, in the 80's, during the day, Warren and Louis said they got a glimpse of one close to camp. On another trip during the 90's, with my daughter Rhonda, I decided to record what sounded like a big owl that was up the ravine about 200 yards. I inadvertently left the recorder's speaker switch in the "on" position, and due to the small microphone pinned to my shirt, a high-pitched squeal fed back. The owl sound immediately turned into Biggie chatter.

Bigfoot was not approaching our camp as before and wasn't vocally interacting anymore. During those years, except for the recordings, these creatures had been crafty enough, seemingly even smart enough, to avoid camera verification. At the time I had no idea how significant the recordings would become. We seemed to continually underestimate Biggie's level of reasoning, thinking of them as very elusive, but unique creatures, and we were just unlucky, or not skillful enough, with our tricks. But after years of interviewing folks, coupled with my involvement with credible Bigfoot enthusiasts, and hearing many accounts, I've concluded that they are likely much more than just an elusive, unidentified great ape running around in the woods. To me, barring any paranormal issues, they seem to live and act more like a primitive people, very much in touch with the environment.

Author and Bill McDowell, 1974

Are they people? That question didn't arise with our group in the 70's. What came from our conversations was the subject of language. The 1974 interaction strongly suggested that they were communicating to each other in a coherent manner, and not just mimicking our sounds or producing vocal displays. Could they be – are they – sentient, self-aware beings?

Problems on the Trail

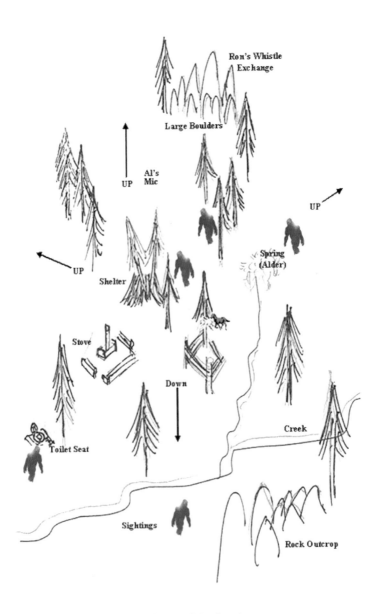

Ron's Whistle
Exchange

Large Boulders

UP

Al's
Mic

UP

UP

Spring
(Alder)

Shelter

Stove

Down

Creek

Toilet Seat

Sightings

Rock Outcrop

Sierra Camp sighting locations

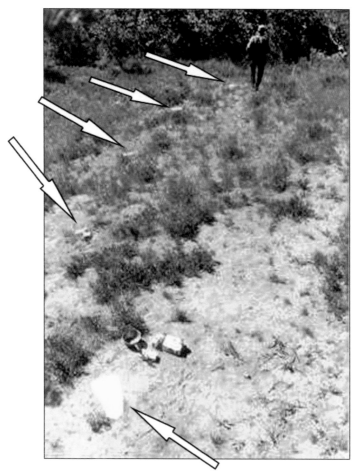

Track casting around the Sierra Camp

Warren Johnson Casting a Bigfoot Track

Chapter 12

More Signs & Sightings

Even though Biggie came in close during the 70's, interacted, and took food from us, I don't think food was the only thing they wanted. I think they may have wanted to know more about us and perhaps wanted us to know something about them. Over those few short years, I believe we gained their trust. The killing of deer didn't seem to bother them – perhaps killing the bear did. The remote location of camp may have contributed to the encounters. Or, if we really want to stretch our imagination, it could have been those sock hats we often wore around camp to keep our heads warm, which may have resembled their sagittal crest. Maybe they thought we were their little pale-faced forest brothers.

It could also be that we were just lucky to have had this remarkable, close-up adventure with Biggie. I stopped hunting this area many years ago, but still trek there during the summer, usually with Rhonda. There have been several reports of Bigfoot sightings within a 20-mile radius of our camp. So apparently others are seeing them, too. I think we may have lost the frequency of their visits because of our actions, or maybe their interest in us just stopped. Or, perhaps there were internal family issues with this particular Bigfoot family. We may never know.

What is known is that they are still around this area and toy with us at times. In the late 90's, Rhonda and I trekked to camp. After a pancake breakfast, we went on a hike, carrying only our lunch in a daypack. I left my large backpack with the remainder of our food by the stove area. Daytime rarely gives us problems with bear, so we were not overly concerned about the food being left out of the shelter. As usual, however, I threw my smelly T-shirt over my backpack and that human smell will often discourage a bear (actually it could discourage anything). When we returned I noticed my T-shirt was placed to the side, and the plastic wrapper from our really good whole grain bread was on the ground. From a full unopened loaf, which had been inside my backpack, not even a crumb was to be found anywhere. None of the other food in my pack was disturbed, and the top flap was closed like it was when we left. These are the type of puzzles that we dealt with around our camp during the 90's. Again, when it comes to food, bears are not that neat.

Unusual reports regarding the elusiveness and mystical aspects of Bigfoot are rumored all the way from Canada to California. The Sierra Nevada mountain range is just one of many mountain ranges in the west. I've been asked several times, "Where is the Sierra camp?" Out of respect for these giants, and the other men involved, I don't reveal the camp's location. I tell folks that I believe our encounters were not necessarily dependent on our area, but the attitude and the demeanor of the sober individuals involved. Bigfoot seems to be curious about human behavior and, for reasons unknown, was apparently curious about us. Knowing what to do when Biggie's tell-tale signs are noticed is not as important as knowing what not to do.

Based on my experience I suggest: 1) If you're lucky enough to see one, don't take your eyes off of it...especially if you hear a scream from another direction. That's difficult, but chances are they are trying to cleverly divert your attention. When you turn around to see what's screaming, the one you were looking at will most likely be gone when you turn back. 2) If you hear a huge limb being snapped, don't jump up and down and shine a flashlight; be still and continue what you're doing. They may come closer if they think they don't have your attention. 3) If you hear them chatter and think it's directed at you, I suggest talking back to them in a calm manner, and refrain from aggressiveness. 4) Don't take dogs with you. It's been reported many times that they have killed dogs that annoy them. Consider taking horses, if you can. Horses don't bark or chase them, and they've actually shown interest in ours. 5) Be sober and cheerful, and have only one or two others with you that have the same demeanor. 6) Wait until some type of activity has taken place prior to setting a camera trap or using recording equipment. 7) Take detailed notes, including weather conditions, food eaten, etc.

You can try all the tricks you want, but they seem to be able to see right through tricks and understand more than most would credit them with. I suggest remaining simple and gaining their trust before trying any 'tricks' at all, like camera traps or recorders. But, don't get too disappointed if your tricks don't work, just back off for a few days.

With that being stated, patience is often easier said than done. Once, from inside the shelter, while Biggie was sounding off, sleep-deprived Louis lost his patience and ended up yelling, "Shut up and go away." The creature came to the shelter, removed an 8-inch, round, dead log, broke it in half and urinated on it. Perhaps he thought he was being yelled at disrespectfully. The Biggie activity was over for that night.

In 1972 Louis was in the shelter watching through a hole which Larry had made earlier and claimed to have seen a gorilla-like creature walking upright. He saw it pass from about 20 feet away, headed toward the stove. With a quiet whisper he said to Larry, "There he is." Larry looked out the opening and also saw something walking upright moving through the brush. It turned and faced the shelter. Larry said the frame looked like that of a football player with all his gear on, no neck and very broad shoulders. It was a bright, moonlit night and no facial features were seen. The next morning they measured the prints. They were 22 inches long and they estimated the height to be about 10 feet.

Late one evening, when the moon was out, Larry was on his way to camp. He claimed to have gotten glimpses of three large shadowy creatures walking upright from about 50 yards away, in and out of a wooded area. They were single-file, in a parallel-type track with him, keeping pace and headed toward our camp.

At dusk, in 1995 while at camp, after we finished our dinner, Rhonda saw a Bigfoot. It was only a moment's glance from about 75 feet away, but a clear view of a broad-shouldered, muscular Bigfoot looking directly at her. It turned and disappeared into the thick forest. She was stunned (it should also be mentioned that she was on her menstrual cycle at the time). I looked up at her and she was pointing toward the creature. "There it is," she finally said. By the time I put my food down, and figured out something unusual was going on, the creature was gone. To top this off, my camera was strapped to a nail 10 feet away. I think the Bigfoot family we were dealing with in the 70's still recognized us during the 90's.

Rhonda (Morehead) O'Connell

Chapter 13

Exploring in 2008

Many sighting reports listed on different websites are in the general region of our camp and are close to an unexplored, imposing area that's actually only about a mile or so, as the crow flies, from our shelter. After noting these reports, and triangulating the locations, I've wanted to explore this area. But getting there would not be easy. I thought it was reasonable to think that this particular family of Bigfoots might use this spot as their home base.

In the summer of 2008, Rhonda and I camped in the vicinity of this area and planned to continue our trip to this very spot the next morning. We set up camp late that evening. As I was preparing the meal, Rhonda left our campfire, went behind a tree and did what she does in private. Just as she returned we both jumped to attention when we heard a loud whoop from about 50 feet away. This was immediately followed by the sound of a huge limb being snapped. Then another whoop came from a distance. The whoops went on for well over an hour that night. This type of behavior was more than reminiscent of the sounds I recorded in the 70's. The sounds were almost exactly the same.

The following day, I retrieved my HD camera, set it on night-shot, and got my recording equipment ready. I used black electrical tape to secure my two black wireless microphones to some trees several feet away – I was having a James Bond moment. Obviously, because of the Biggie activity, we didn't want to leave this spot, so we were ready for action that night. As we lay there in our sleeping bags, with my finger ready to push the button on the recorder, there was total silence. Nothing was happening. I began sensing the serenity of the quiet forest, my tired eyes slowly dropped, and I drifted off to sleep. The next morning Rhonda said she heard distant whoops throughout the night. Could it have been owls? Maybe, but I'm quite certain the whoops from the previous night weren't. Owls are not able to produce that much amplitude, and I'm certain they couldn't have snapped that log. I shouldn't have set up all my fancy equipment – too complicated, too soon. Will I ever learn?

It's easy to get excited and forget the importance of staying simple and predictable around these creatures. Our time had run out and another trip was needed, plus a firm-reminder that "patience is a virtue", especially when dealing with Biggie. This is an attribute that I think some Bigfoot researchers should have more of. Many misguided enthusiasts drive to the end of a logging road, pull out their boom-box, crack open a six-pack, and start blasting the Sierra recordings. I suppose it's fun, and probably an enjoyable way to spend the weekend, but usually unproductive. Be simple, be patient, and let them make the first move. Plus, we don't know what those sounds represent. Biggie might be looking for a mate and blasting those sounds might encourage an undesirable response – you've been warned.

Bill McDowell casting footprints in the snow

Chapter 14

Getting A Professional On Board

Science refers to a system of acquiring knowledge. It requires organizing thoughts and procedures. Good science should never be predicated on one's likes or dislikes, personal beliefs or disbeliefs, or unsupported whimsical assumptions. Human arrogance or jealousy has no place in this discipline. Most scientists have worked hard to obtain their credentials and will not take a chance on losing their credibility (or their job) by pursuing such a topic as Bigfoot. Perhaps if we would get away from the cartoonish sound of Bigfoot, Wildman or Yeti, they will take the subject more seriously. Most of them will not professionally acknowledge the existence of these creatures, but, on a personal level, believe they most likely exist. The many reports from credible eyewitnesses cannot all be mischievously contrived. Some, however, could be mistaken. Bears can, and sometimes do, walk on two feet. However, as they walk they also leave paw-prints. Bigfoot leaves big footprints and these prints are factual evidence to science.

The discipline of science should always be respected. But does classical science go far enough? Have the few scientists working in this Bigfoot field considered all the arrows they have in their scientific quiver; specifically, have they considered quantum physics and how it may relate to the enigma associated with Bigfoot? Quantum physics is a remarkable phenomenon. As it stands now conventional, or classical, science demands facts that support a hypothesis, similar to a courtroom verdict. However, quantum physics has its own dilemma, which, without a doubt, is challenging to anyone.

In October of 2011, I was invited to participate in a conference being held in Russia. The Russians have a more scientific name for the study of their Snowman or Yeti; it's referred to as 'hominology' and those that study it are hominologists. They suggest the creature be referred to as a homin. The interest in my experiences, from the media, the Russian hominologists, and even their government, was exciting to me. There were two PhDs that joined me, one from the USA and another from Canada. They have both heard my presentation before, so I wasn't surprised when there were no questions from them, even when we were alone. However, it seems my 40 years dealing with this mystery should have been of more interest. I have a huge amount of respect for the effort, dedication, and time it takes to acquire the scientific discipline and achieve their level of knowledge.

But, to me, the American-based scientists seem to have made up their minds regarding the genus of these beings, much of which is based on the evidence in existence, the actual footprints these creatures leave, not so much the documented vocalizations, which I think should have captured more attention.

For our recordings to attain an accepted level of credibility scientists must be involved – and in an unbiased way. The recordings we made in the Sierra Nevada Mountains command all that classical science can muster, yet the approach must also include open-mindedness. Scientists should consider all the reports they have at their disposal, not discard them because they don't fit into their discipline, or their paradigm. It seems to me that they are working with checkers when they could be playing chess.

To get to the bottom of the *Sierra Sounds* we needed a qualified expert to take them on and establish what our recordings from the 70's represent. Al Berry has two degrees in science, one is a Masters, and it's not easy to bluff him in that field – or any field as far as that goes. He sought a scientific analysis to credit (or discredit) the recordings, either way, just so it would give us a professional, unbiased report.

After several disappointing rejections, Al found Professor R. Lynn Kirlin, at the University of Wyoming. In 1978, he and a student, Lasse Hertel, carried out a year-long, semi-quantitative study which gave our recordings unbiased scientific credibility. The conclusion of his analysis was presented at an academic symposium convened in Vancouver, British Columbia, entitled *Anthropology of the Unknown* and also published in a book by the University of British Columbia Press, entitled *Manlike Monsters on Trial.*

Dr. Kirlin summarized his findings with the following:

Having analyzed a tape recording of purported Bigfoot speech using accepted techniques of signal processing, the authors conclude that the means and ranges of the recorded pitch and estimated vocal tract length of the speakers indicate that the sounds were made by a creature with "vocal features corresponding to a larger physical size than man." They also conclude that the tape shows none of the expected signs of being prerecorded or rerecorded at altered speed and hence diminish the probability of a hoax.

His report also stated:

If Bigfoot is actually proven to exist, the vocalizations on these tapes may well be of great anthropological value, being a unique observation of Bigfoot in his natural environment.

Professor Kirlin's work was a huge step forward for the Bigfoot craze happening in the Pacific Northwest and also for the Sierra recordings. But it was not enough to seize the level of professional attention we thought they deserved. So our search continued.

Dr. R. Lynn Kirlin

Nancy Logan is a human sound expert and had the position as the only interpreter in the State of California who was court certified in Spanish/English and Japanese/English and court registered in French/English. Besides the languages she speaks, she also has studied others, such as Chinese and Arabic, is known to have perfect pitch, and also apparently speaks these languages without an accent. Ms. Logan listened to our recordings intensely during the early 90's and wrote the following:

I believe that some sort of primitive communication is going on in the form of primitive language. The first time I listened to the tapes, I thought it was linguistically a little more sophisticated than I do now. After listening to them again, I think that the creatures are a little more animal sounding, but I still think it is language. I challenge anyone to make those exact same noises with the exact same pronunciation and intonation at that speed.

It would take an incredible amount of training for a human to make these noises so fluently and spontaneously. The noises also include vocalizations made with what sounds like parts of their vocal tract that native English speakers would have tremendous trouble in learning. They are trying to communicate with you.

Although Ms. Logan gave her professional opinion as a human sound expert, our recorded primate sounds were still begging for attention into the late 90's. Al and I wrote letters to several universities, hoping a qualified professional would take on our project, but we received very little response. What response we did receive was biased and obviously emitted a component of silent snickering. Once a highly respected bio-acoustical firm said if we would pay them $5,000.00 "in advance," they would let us know what made the sounds in three days, a little too good to be true. We didn't take the bait and they didn't get our money.

As we continued to look for professional input, I noticed an article in a well-liked and very popular magazine. The title was, "Inside Animal Minds," and it quoted the following from the Great Ape Trust Research in Iowa: Kanzi, a bonobo, is supposedly learning English. "We think he may be speaking English words, just too fast and high-pitched for us to decode," (William M. Field, National Geographic, May 2008).

That article leaped out at me – "... too fast and high-pitched for us to decode?" It sounded strangely familiar. For several years a lady has been contacting me and claiming that she can understand what these creatures are saying. She said that they are trying to speak English. For years I could not bring myself to entertain that notion, but now I wonder. Over a time line of perhaps centuries, could they have actually picked up English and/ or Native American phrases by listening to human conversations around campfires? I used to wonder, "Do they understand what they're saying or just mimic what they hear?" The speed at which they talk, can be incredibly fast.

Play Soundtrack (23)

These rapid-fire sounds have been a notably divisive issue with some "wannabe" Bigfoot enthusiasts. The chatter seemed to be difficult for many to handle and was undoubtedly the topic of many campfire discussions. Public curiosity about the recordings needed to be addressed.

To answer some of these questions Al and I decided to make a CD of the story and the sounds. Al wrote his account in 1996 and I produced the first CD, The Bigfoot Recordings. He encouraged me to write my account using the interactive sounds that I recorded two years later, but it wasn't until 2003 that I produced that CD, The Bigfoot Recordings Volume II. Sharing our stories, with integrated creature vocalizations, could bring about the attention we thought they deserved. The more interest we could engage, the better.

For the record, and at the suggestion of a scientist from an animal sounds investigative facility in North Carolina (Fauna Communications Research Institute), Al and I decided it would be good to have a thorough assessment of the flora and fauna to document the surroundings of our camp.

Joe Hauser, Wildlife biologist

We asked Joe Hauser, a wildlife biologist, to contact Fauna Communications and find out exactly what type of information they would like in the assessment. In addition to reporting on the fauna and flora, Mr. Hauser was also given the task of checking for any signs of possible hoaxing or devious activities. Mr. Hauser had previously contacted Al and me regarding some unusually large feces which had been masticated that he found in the mountains. That defecation was also associated with some very unusual yells that he'd heard and couldn't identify.

Mr. Hauser is a tremendous outdoors man and a survivalist, too. He has even taught classes on that subject. He and I hiked to our camp so he could carry out his analysis. An interesting item that I recall about Mr. Hauser's investigation was that he found river rocks that had been carried to an area near our camp – they had been put in a small pile behind a large rock outcropping. No person in his or her right mind would bring rocks that distance. Hauling anything up to that remote area without a purpose would be ludicrous, especially rocks. Could these rocks be the ones that were being popped together in the 70's?

75

Although I had noticed these rocks in the past, it never dawned on me that they were not from that area. Joe Hauser was like a walking encyclopedia. Every tree, every bush and every rock was a wealth of information, and he shared it with me. He presented his findings in an article entitled "Sierra Deer Camp Investigation."* (complete report, pg. 125) http://www.bigfootsounds.com/index.php/feed/ Mr. Hauser's knowledge of the forest was also complemented by his knowledge of the Native Americans – it seemed unlimited. He talked about the natives' diets, he braided rope from wild grass, and started a fire with a couple of sticks and a string. "At one time Native Americans were surely in this area," he said. After he made the exhausting trip and explored the area for three days, he listened to my story and I think became more enthusiastic about the Bigfoot phenomenon.

Lots of folks are interested in the subject. The encounters I had were (and still are) an amazing experience, but also a continually frustrating one. Al and I still needed a different type of professional to get involved. How could we get a qualified person to take an unbiased view of our story and study these unusual primate sounds? Over the years, we kept open an invitation for any expert skilled at interpreting unusual sounds – an expert that had access to modern technology and would contribute their expertise for a full-blown study. We needed to get this "burr" out of our saddle.

It finally happened in March 2008 when Scott Nelson contacted me. He is retired from Naval Intelligence as a Crypto-Linguist and teaches Russian, Spanish and Persian at a college in Missouri. He asked if he could listen to, and perhaps study, the original recordings.

Having logged thousands of hours of voice transcription, claiming perfect pitch, trained by the military to decipher codes, Mr. Nelson thought he heard language within the sound bites he'd heard.

After thoroughly interviewing Al and me regarding the context and circumstances surrounding the sounds, Scott and his team went to work on the original recordings. We couldn't have asked for someone more qualified. After several months of intense and detailed work Mr. Nelson released the following statement:

We have verified that these creatures use language, by the human definition of it. The months of hard work that we have put into the study of the Berry/Morehead tapes is finally coming to fruition. The analysis is finished, although I am still working on parts of the final write-up such as frequency count tables, morpheme lists, etc.

I believe that the study of these tapes will never (and should never) end. With the recognition and acceptance that these creatures do indeed speak and understand a complex language, a greater effort will be made to collect voice recordings and our analysis of the language will improve. Now that we have a precedent and techniques established for this study, this process will certainly become easier.

Since Mr. Nelson stepped forward with his statement he has been inundated with folks sending him recordings believed to be those of Bigfoot – many of which are interesting, but not of the quality needed for study. In 2007, during a mini expedition in Ohio led by Mark Maisel, David Donlon captured sounds that were remarkably similar to the Sierra recordings. Al Berry and I originally thought those sounds must have been plagiarized from our recordings. However, I personally went through all the sounds that we've released to the public and they did not match.

Play Soundtrack (24)

By claiming he found complex language imbedded within our recordings, Scott stuck his professional neck out and joined the ranks of other educators who have publicly renounced much of their earlier skepticism regarding the Bigfoot phenomenon.

Throughout the winter of 2008, Scott Nelson and I continued to communicate. During his trip to California that December, he impressed Al and me with his ability to mimic several of the sounds we'd recorded. He couldn't mimic the rapid chatter at its original speed but by slowing the recordings down he was able to get very close to sounding like these big guys. Many years ago, Al sent the recordings to a professor for review.

The professor accused Al of speeding up human sounds to pull a trick on him. That shows how these recordings were being received by many professionals. Seeing as how Al was there and originally thought it was most likely a hoax, that didn't set too well with him. The shoe was on the other foot now.

Scott and I decided it would be good to venture all the way into the imposing area where I've wanted to go for years. We had a mission; it was to obtain a video of a Bigfoot talking. With his unique vocal ability, coupled with my experience around these beings, and my knowledge of the area, perhaps we'd be successful.

R. Scott Nelson

Chapter 15

Seeking Corroboration

My original animal pack team has long since gone to horse and mule heaven, but I formed another. My attempt to step back into the past and create some significant and adventuresome Bigfoot interaction had begun. This undertaking could also mark the beginning of a very important chapter in the long-enduring Sierra Sounds story.

For us to stay in the woods for several weeks we would need a pack team to haul all our stuff...taking quick trips out for needed supplies, eliminating a few necessary business demands, and perhaps getting an essential hot shower. However, we need to stay as long as we can each time. I think Bigfoot needs to get used to any change in the environment that humans make and to trust the people involved if there is to be any productive interaction. I also think habituating an area is very important to accomplish the goal of learning about these beings.

First, I purchased Maddy, a 22-year-old Pinto mare. Her horse-age was old, she was a bit stuck in her ways, but still in fair shape, and hopefully strong enough to pack our stuff. She could also save on the weed-whacking time at my home in Mariposa. Secondly, I found an Arabian gelding, Jack. He looked almost exactly like JR. For me this was an omen, and I just had to buy that horse. Arabians are beautiful to look at, are bred for endurance, and have lots of energy. However, coupling Jack with Maddy could be problemati,; too much energy with an Arabian and not enough with Maddy. Plus, JR was only 'half' Arabian, Jack was full-blooded. I was in good physical shape but 'twice' the age; another potential energy-imbalance problem. However, I still planned to wrangle Maddy while riding Jack up to this commanding part of the Sierras. Jack may have to pull Maddy most of the way, but he's strong and could probably use something to hold him back. I also purchased a beautiful black quarter horse mare called Mo – Scott could ride her. There they were, Maddy, Mo and Jack (Pep Boys pun not intended).

However, from a practice run, loaded with unimportant stuff, it was obvious that my dream-team was not balanced and just wasn't going to pan out. Mo didn't like other horses too close to her, Jack was full of nervous energy and Maddy was just tired all the time. So I came to my senses, and a couple weeks before Scott was to join me I bought a guaranteed trail-ready quarter horse...Moon. This horse's demeanor was very much like Mo's, and their get-up-and-go level seemed to be about the same – a good pair. Jack would have to stay home for now, and hopefully Maddy would be able to keep up.

Jack

Mo

Maddy & Jack at Author's Ranch

The summer of 2009 came. Scott was on sabbatical from his teaching job in Missouri, I had the horses, a horse trailer and, yup...another cowboy hat. Within this short period of time, Jack and Maddy had become very bonded, almost inseparable. As we loaded Mo, Moon and Maddy, Jack was left pacing the fence. The word "pacing" is probably an understatement. I think his mind had previously been exclusive on processing hay, but had obviously changed to an envious, nervous, and "uh oh" thought of, "Where are you taking my soul mate?" The horses were settling into the trailer, and after loading the remainder of our supplies, Scott and I pulled out for the high country. For a while I continued to look for Jack in my rearview mirror.

The trail up the switchbacks had not been used that year and there was no one available to give me a heads-up on its condition. The winter's snow runoff, trees that fall across the trail, and the sheer imposing terrain can make for some real excitement when you're on horseback. We set up camp at the trailhead, which allowed the animals to acclimate to the lighter air of the high country and would also allow for an early start the next morning. The weather was perfect and when daybreak came we drank a quick cup of coffee, saddled up the horses, packed Maddy and got on the trail. But, after hours of absolute tribulation, the trip was brought to an inopportune halt. To say the least, these flat-lander, valley-trained, parade-perfect animals had their problems with this trail, and consequently I had my hands full. It appeared the Good Mountain gods were on a break that day. This rugged switchback trail with its slick boulders, exposed tree roots, and an occasional rattlesnake, requires veteran, mountain-seasoned, rootin'-tootin' animals, which I didn't have. And probably could have used a younger carefree wrangler, which I wasn't. This mountain adventure, and the potential for a new connection with Bigfoot, was not working out.

The first time I felt the need to abandon the saddle was when Maddy decided to turn back at the first switchback. Trying to hold on to her made no sense at all, but I did and Moon slipped off the edge. I've been there and done this before, so I voluntarily decided to take my chances and pick my spot to land. Unfortunately, I landed on my wrist. A rapidly swelling wrist makes it almost impossible to hold on to a lead-rope. One hand on the reins, and one hand being cautiously guarded, adds to the challenge of those twists and turns. A few switchbacks later, Maddy lost her footing. I was walking, leading Moon, but Maddy's lead rope was around his saddle horn. The sight of those horses going head-over-hooves down that grade was definitely film-worthy and reminiscent of the old days with JR and Rabbit – except without me on board.

I spent the best part of a couple of hours picking up supplies from the mountainside, gathering up the horses, and repacking Maddy. Scott and Mo were ahead of me on their own wild adventure ride and didn't see any of this. It just isn't in one's nature to back-track after accomplishing so much up that trail. However, after so much time passing, Scott knew something must have gone wrong and came back – a welcomed sight. It was really becoming a struggle to load those packs on Maddy, but thanks to Scott, we got it done.

However, during all the gathering of supplies, there was a golden moment when I found one of our unbroken melons and decided to take a break, eat it and let my feet rest. I ate only half and left the other half for the birds, the non-nut-gathering squirrels, or maybe a hungry "something". This melon issue became an interesting topic for a short discussion with Scott a few hours later.

But, the "last hurrah" for the day was later, when Mo froze in her tracks. No matter how hard Scott kicked her she wouldn't move (I should have given him spurs). That's when Maddy and Moon had time to think about how hard this trip was and decided to head back again. With only one good hand and broken reins, I had no dominating control whatsoever and saw another calamity in the making. With a smooth leap, I voluntarily abandoned the saddle (again) and spent another hour trekking back down to get those horses; "I can't let them get away with all this," I said to Scott. When I finally caught up to Scott again, he reminded me how late it was. That's when I knew we were not going to find the campsite before dark. So, with mishap after mishap, and the realization that we couldn't get where I wanted to go, we headed back down the trail. Something was definitely bothering those horses besides the imposing trail. It may have been a disturbed bear, maybe a restless mountain lion, or...or...or, just possibly, a curious Bigfoot.

As we headed back, Maddy was on her own about 100 yards ahead, peering around the boulders, whinnying as loud as she could for the other horses. I was leading Moon past a very slippery spot when my feet, which were wrapped in cowboy boots, told me, "We'd really rather ride." As I began to mount Moon, he decided that he didn't want to be ridden and may have thought Maddy needed him more than I did. I was halfway in the saddle when he took off running and bucking. I knew my time in this predicament was rapidly coming to an end. But, this time I had no choice of a landing spot. Scott had the privilege of witnessing this rodeo event and said that I must have sailed fifteen feet in the air. After seeing all this, he said that his first thought was how to get Ron's dead body off that mountain prior to nightfall; otherwise, the bears may want him for dinner and the kids would never forgive him. But, to his surprise, after he got to me, he heard me moaning. "I'm not dead," I mumbled between breaths, "just help me up before I start swelling and can't walk." I was lucky. I landed on a sandy area between two large boulders. However, as one could observe by their skinned-up hide and the broken tack, the horses surely got the worst of it all. I ended the day with a sprained wrist, a cracked rib and bruised pride – I also remember the ground being much softer years ago.

But, as we continued down the trail we came across that half melon I'd left for the animals. I left it about 50 feet away from the trail, where I finished eating the other half. The melon was cleaned out, yet the rind was complete. A bird couldn't have carried it that far; a bear would have eaten the rind too, and a deer couldn't have done this either. We were taking those melons for an offering to Biggie. Maybe he somehow knew we weren't gonna make it to camp that day and took his snack early. That day, Scott and I must have looked like the *two-stooge pack team*.

Scott was invaluable when it came to loading the animals in the trailer, driving my truck, and helping me with my boots. With a cracked rib, my laughing was definitely curtailed, and heaven forbid if I sneezed or coughed. But our trip and the excitement weren't over.

Rhonda had been told that she could not go with us because Biggie needed to get used to Scott with minimal distractions. Rhonda was left out of the "cowboy club" and was feeling a bit miffed. Not to be deprived, she had set up camp about 12 miles from the trailhead. She convinced her mother and Wendy, my 18-year-old granddaughter, to join her. It was a welcome spot for Scott and me to informally crash their camp for a couple days. Every bump in the road tormented me, but perhaps with a couple of days rest, I'd be better for the long trip home. The girls fixed our meals, set up a spare tent for us, and fortunately had something for my pain. Scott took off hiking into the woods and exerted his mimicking talent. As the crow flies, this area was only about 2 miles from my Biggie hot spot. It's very inhospitable for humans to trek in that direction, and impossible for horses or mules to navigate the cliffs and boulders. Plus, from reviewing the BFRO website * (www.bfro.net), I saw that there were several other reports coming out of this area.

The BFRO has an excellent site. They post and categorize Bigfoot sightings, along with valuable information for Bigfoot enthusiasts.

Scott Nelson on Mo, Trailhead 2009

Scott's vocal skills paid off on the second night. At about 2 a.m., the girls were awakened by the huge sound of something crashing through the trees. Immediately afterward, with a force that "Sounded like a two-legged elephant," Rhonda said something walked to behind the tent, stopped and grunted. They claimed it milled around for about 45 minutes, putting out repeated grunts. Could it have been a bear? They didn't think so.

At one time they thought it was coming *through* the tent. Spooked by the event, and their gripping urge to urinate, the girls felt compelled to get up and out of the tent. Whatever was making those troublesome sounds stopped, and the girls spent the remainder of the night hunkered around the campfire.

With the help of those pills, I slept soundly through the whole thing but, when daybreak came, Rhonda stuck her head in our tent and with a startled voice said, "I just saw a Bigfoot"; that awakened me. She said that it was coming from the creek, briskly walking across an opening, headed up that steep mountainside – and "yes", running on two feet. Trying very hard to keep her composure, she couldn't stop talking about the inhuman-like gait. And that night something or someone had placed a small log behind their tent: a gift meant for the fire perhaps? Bears don't do that.

Scott said that during the night he felt what seemed like a large hand pressing against the tent onto his sleeping bag, and it definitely had not been the girls. Unbeknownst to Scott, a few years earlier at our Sierra camp, Rhonda told me of a similar incident that she experienced while we were sleeping outside the shelter. Over the years, during eyewitness interviews, I've heard other claims of this happening. While in Siberia I was fortunate enough to hear from a lady who reported the exact same occurrence, but she witnessed the creature walking away. Obviously, there's some kind of commonality about it, but what does it mean?

That morning as I looked out of the tent's opening, Mo was on her back with all four legs sticking straight up in the air. I've never seen a horse, that wasn't dead, like that – a definite Kodak moment, but I didn't even think of a camera at the time. She was, however, still tied to the picket-line. But, Maddy wasn't – she was loose. The snap-hook on Maddy's halter is the type that doesn't easily come undone – it takes an opposable thumb. The situation was actually comical in appearance, but I really couldn't laugh yet. The events of that morning did, however, put us all in a state of wonderment of what really went on during the night.

Everyone wanted to stay longer, but I was stiff and sore and it was my call. We broke camp, loaded the animals, and began our journey back to the valley. Scott spent a couple of nights at my house and then returned to his home and family in Missouri. Our 2009 summer plan to habituate an area and obtain video of a Bigfoot talking had ended for that year. Perhaps we had set the bar too high.

Deep impressions behind campsite, Scott, Rhonda and Wendy

Scott Nelson compares stride

Maddy, Moon and Mo: Picket-line for horses

Author

Chapter 16

2010 Excursion

Scott returned to California in the summer of 2010. He and I spoke at a symposium in Oregon and then headed for California's high country again. This time we made a plan to backpack, a much wiser thing to do, especially since (again) I didn't know the condition of the trail. Determined to capture more corroborative evidence of Bigfoot, we packed enough supplies to last a few weeks. Although I had made it clear to Scott that the whereabouts of our Bigfoot occurrences was not to be revealed, I had reservations about taking him to our shelter. Instead, we set up camp about one mile away. This spot is also closer to the spot I've wanted to explore for some time. At daybreak the following morning we began the strenuous walk to this almost inaccessible area. It was obvious that there was not going to be an easy way to get into this "bowl" with its cliff walls and dense forest. It's good the days are long in June, but this day was not long enough. Actually, it was also clear that in order to access this area it would be an overnighter and we needed to have a better plan.

Back at camp, while I was digging a hole for our 'private reading area' (mini-throne), the small fold-up shovel collapsed and I strained my Achilles tendon. It was apparent that I needed a "handicapped" sign hanging around my neck. So early the next morning we secured camp, wrapped our remaining supplies in a tarp and hoisted them high in a tree. I got a walking stick, and we spent the next day trying to get out before dark. Back home, healing came quickly so we returned in late July. To help with our supply concerns I took Mo. She's good for riding or packing, she's okay without the other horses along, and it would make my part of the trip much easier – especially with a weak ankle. The trip in went well, we broke open camp and got settled in.

That afternoon Scott rhythmically beat on a small drum and we immediately heard mimicking sounds being returned from each side of our camp. Late at night I was awakened by chatter, coming from about 75 feet away. Of course, I didn't get my recorder turned on in time to capture those sounds. They actually stopped when I was trying to turn it on, as if they could see the small red recording light I was fumbling with in my sleeping bag. I then lay quietly in my sleeping bag with my recorder in hand, but drifted off to sleep – it happens. While on the trip out I was ahead of Scott by about 100 yards when I heard powerful, startling cries of some type (not the sound of a bear) coming from the woods, about 75 feet away. The interesting part was my horse's attention was concentrated on the opposite side of the trail, not in the direction of the sounds – possibly due to a diversionary ploy?

A memorable adventure, but we certainly didn't acquire the data we'd wanted. We did, however, make a significant move in the right direction, and I think made a positive connection. Scott was slowly being accepted by Biggie, and I heard their sounds – however, Scott didn't. I should continually try to learn from my efforts and mistakes, let them be the instigator, and change as little as possible in the environment. Again -- it must be on their time and under their terms.

Author, 2011, Sierra Camp

Chapter 17

40 Years in the Wilderness

2011

It was July 2011, and I had just spoken at another symposium in Oregon; Scott was on his way from Missouri to meet me in California. Another trip to the high country was in the works. As in previous years, information about the trail was not available so we backpacked. This greatly reduced the potential of a horse mishap, but also demanded a weight restriction on our supplies.

My plan was to go without a camera, a recorder or a gun to see if any of that made a difference. However, after due consideration, I took a small .22 caliber handgun with bird shot. If necessary this little butt-stinger will ward off a bear if he becomes too comfortable with the smell of our food. Either that or he'll really get pissed off. Scott had acquired a new digital recorder and took enough batteries to record 24 hours a day for several days.

To help with our supply concern, Scott brought his 14-year-old son. Like a Billy goat with a backpack, he tromped up that mountain a whole lot easier than we did. After four days with no Biggie action and no food left (teenagers can really eat a lot), we hiked out, took a shower, resupplied and then returned with his 28-year-old daughter; also in good shape, she helped with more supplies and didn't eat nearly as much as his son. After four more days we hiked out again, showered, resupplied and the two of us walked back in for a third time – now that's conditioning.

The only excitement was when Scott and I jumped a huge bear that we stumbled across on the trail. Scott's immediate concern was the gun; "Where's the gun?" he asked. It was comfortably stowed away in my backpack. "No need for the gun," I said, "he'll run away when he gets wind of us." I wanted to watch this bear for a while, but Scott didn't like the idea of him slowly grazing toward us. The bear was getting a bit too close so Scott began making noise and the bear took off. But, within 30 minutes another big one ran across the trail in front of us. The size of the bears, the size of my handgun, and the concern about our food (and my ass) gave me pause – those two bears were big! Would my little gun be enough to discourage that size bear? Maybe not, but it was the risk that I took. It's a great feeling for me, however, when I get to observe wildlife for a while before they catch on to me and run away. The weather was fabulous on all three trips. However, there was no Biggie activity whatsoever. We could only speculate as to the reason.

It could have been that these hairy giants were just not around. It's also possible that Biggie wasn't comfortable with the new personalities or, perhaps, the different atmosphere around camp. We were not there to hunt deer, but to capture more of Bigfoot's vocalizations. Also, we planned to leave food for them, but the bacon smelled so good, we ate it ourselves.

The month of July had come and gone and I realized that this mountain and its curious inhabitants had captured me for 40 years. And I still don't have answers as to what these giants are. Our mission was incomplete and, for one reason or another, our quest for significant corroboration was held up again.

It was the end of August, the Good-Weather gods were still blessing the Sierras, and I really wanted to know if the big guys were up there or not. So, I decided to do something that I hadn't done since the 70's, something stupid, irresponsible, and somewhat arrogant. I decided to walk into camp alone and see if that would stir something up – something besides the deer, bear and squirrels. This time I took my recorder, my camera and a bigger .38 caliber handgun with bird shot. If I had a problem holding on to my food around camp, it would sting that big bear much better than the questionable .22.

The three trips that Scott and I made in July got my lungs and legs in good shape, so I wasn't worried about conditioning. However, as in the 70's, some of the same reasons for not going alone were working on my head, like accidents, nobody to corroborate anything that might happen, and so on. But those reasons didn't stop me. I packed enough food for three days and, after spending the night at the bottom of that mountain, left the next morning. I arrived in camp early in the afternoon, broke open the shelter, and set up a small tent close to the stove area. The snow load from the winter had taken its toll on the roof of the shelter and it didn't look safe. Bear had also rummaged in the area but most everything was still intact.

Bear in 2011

As mentioned, on this trip the Good-Weather gods were with me; however, the Evil Little Mosquito gods were, too. In the past those little blood-suckers had never been much of a problem, but this time they were. For a brief moment I considered using my gun on them. I was being overwhelmed, but thought it wise to not try to take them out with the bird shot – only had 3 of them anyway.

At 6:00 p.m., with no repellent on hand, I went inside the tent, zipped it up and started reading. The forest was extremely quiet; my blood level had regenerated just in time. It was 6:15 when an attention-getting wood knock rang out from just outside my tent. I would compare the amplitude to a gunshot – very loud with a defined purpose that really got my heart pumping. It was completely unexpected, but, thanks to my past experiences, I didn't overreact. I think they wanted to see what I was going to do about that knock and I was determined to be cool. After 15 more minutes I thought it was time to go outside. While using a small white towel to continually ward off the mosquitoes, I began talking to whatever was there. I must have appeared to have been waving a surrender towel. As clearly as I could, I explained that if they wanted to befriend me, I needed to see them before it got dark...and they'd better not scare me after it was dark.

Well, that didn't work. I went into the tent at 7:30 (about dusk), zipped it up, set my recorder on pause, and began to read again. At 10:00 p.m., while I was comfortably lying in my sleeping bag (it was really dark then), I heard some Biggie chatter from approximately 100 feet away. That was immediately followed by an attention-getting thump on an old barrel we use for trash that was about 15 feet from me. My heart was racing as I listened to footsteps cautiously walk around the stove area. "I told you not to scare me after dark!" I yelled. Those steps came up to the tent and paused within a couple feet of me. I could hear breathing, and I have to admit, I was a bit petrified; I couldn't speak and didn't move. I never heard it leave, but I'm sure it did.

Making notes of events when they happen is important and I had been taking notes since I arrived. However, I didn't want to turn on my head lamp any more than necessary – that could put them off. I fumbled for a moment but then found the recorder, pushed the record button, but the new lithium batteries were dead, I suppose from being on pause all that time. I had actually bought them the previous year but hadn't used them. I have no answer for that; they should have still held a charge. I thought I was prepared to capture sounds again; needless to say, I was disappointed.

Other questionable sounds were being emitted during the night and what little sleep I got was less than sound. It was 4:00 a.m., still eerily quiet and pitch black, when I was alerted to rhythmic wood knocking from a distance. It was immediately followed by a high-pitched electronic sound just outside my tent.

That was it. My plan to stay two nights changed to one. As soon as daylight hit, I came out of the tent only to get attacked by those blood-suckers again. Fighting the mosquitoes was just too much, so I closed camp and headed out. Then it dawned on me, I hadn't left any food out for Biggie that night. Maybe that's something he wanted. However, my mission was complete and my question had been answered...Biggie was still around - another reminder that the odds have to be in their favor, they still toy with our heads, and they've got to be in charge.

Chapter 18

Let's Get With It

Sound blast and bellow out all your favorite Bigfoot cries. Why not get out in the woods and get this show on the road? From a distance, one "might" get a yell back, maybe even see a couple red eyeballs peering through the trees, or perhaps hear something crashing through the brush. But, no interaction... why? What we humans do to stir something up just doesn't seem to get much accomplished. Not being able to "make" an encounter happen on our terms is frustrating. The whole Bigfoot issue is like trying to nail Jell-O to the wall, it takes patience and often plays head-games on the "make-it-happen" person. I think too many folks hear a sound in the woods that they can't recognize, immediately jump to conclusions, and overreact. However, there are also the ones that run into would-be evidence and don't recognize it as such. Many red-neck hunters are completely unwilling to accept that a hairy, giant, ape-like being could be in the forest with them. Why? Because they've never seen one. And, of course, if one were out there, they surely would have seen it by now. Much of our belief today is, "If you can't see it, touch it, or smell it, it doesn't exist." But it's a fact that giants have inhabited the Western Hemisphere in the past and I know a type of giant inhabits the Sierras now – I, along with many others, have experienced it.

Except for the human-like and intelligent-looking facial expressions, which I've heard of many times, and their size, Bigfoot appears for the most part more like a big orangutan, long arms, sagittal crest, and hairy. So, hopefully, we are on our way to understanding more about a hair-covered seven-to-ten-foot-tall being that comfortably lives and stealthily roams the forest without the need, or want, of anything we humans take for granted. Bu is that all they are?

All animals have basic, often very unique, instincts for survival. Over time they adapt to overcome environmental changes and life threatening hurdles. We accept survival traits in many animals, the olfactory sense in dogs and bears, echolocation in bats, sonar in whales and dolphins, or a shark's ability to smell blood in water from a very long distance. Tigers use their keen stereo-hearing (along with their excellent sight) to home in on prey, or to avoid humans. They easily find their next meal yet still remain so elusive it takes a huge effort (by means of a lot of patience) to even catch sight of one when actively looking. I have spent days on the ground, and on elephants, following tiger tracks in Nepal. These majestic animals do not have the level of self-awareness that humans have. They don't know that they are leaving tracks and other signs... but what if they did understand? We would probably only see one by accident, or perhaps never – sound familiar?

Unlike the tiger, I think Bigfoot knows they leave signs (tracks), which mean they are self-aware, maybe even more than many care to imagine. That being said, I don't think all my Biggie experiences can be answered by "normal" animal attributes or self-awareness alone – not the kind most of us understand anyway. Perhaps we need to raise the bar on our expectations regarding these creatures. Maybe even ask scientists to take a very special leap, a distinct seismic shift from tradition, and consider that other "arrow" in their quiver, the arrow usually kept away from the bow. But, again, will they? Can they?

Author observing fresh tiger tracks in Nepal

Should our conventional scientists cross traditional boundaries to an interdisciplinary field? Wow! What a question. Accepted worldwide in the 1920's, quantum physics is a science, but its boundaries are not defined and very difficult to understand. It violates some of the accepted properties of classical science and challenges our culture's perception of reality. With all the reports claiming very unusual circumstances surrounding Bigfoot, mine being one, why not consider quantum physics?

Maybe, just maybe, Bigfoot has another survival attribute that we don't understand yet – an attribute that might run "head on" into a quantum field. If these giants are part human, as has been suggested, how closely related to us are they? Could they have come from the same genus *Homo*? Could we humans have actually lost, or separated ourselves from, a survival attribute that we may have had at one time, but still remained rational and self-aware? Ever heard of the Garden of Eden and the apple? What did we actually lose, or get separated from, in that garden when we ate that metaphoric apple? And how might we get it back?

Like a giant puzzle, we're coming across anecdotal information and historical data that seems to flash a picture in front of us. Let's take a deeper look down this rabbit hole and see what we can flush out. Could there be any giants down that little hole?

The Aztecs and Mayans in Central America recorded their encounters with a race of giants to the north when they ventured out on exploratory expeditions. Augustan history records that Maximinus Thrax, the 27th emperor of Rome, who ruled that Empire from 235 to 238 AD, was eight feet, ten inches tall.

In February and June of 1931, large skeletons were found in the Humboldt lake bed, close to Lovelock, Nevada. The first of these two skeletons found measured eight and one half feet tall and appeared to have been wrapped in a gum-covered fabric similar to the Egyptian method. The second skeleton was almost ten feet long (Review - Miner, June 19, 1931). Like so many, these artifacts have mysteriously disappeared.

In a story told by Sarah Winnemucca Hopkins, around 1880, the Paiute Natives in the Lovelock area warred with the Si-Te-Cah, who were cannibals and had red hair. The story goes that they fought until they had killed all but a few who hid in a cave. When the cave was being mined in 1911 the remnants of these red-haired people were reportedly found. Most of the artifacts were lost over time due to lack of interest from science. Some reports indicate they were gigantic in size. Among the artifacts found was a sandal measuring fifteen inches long.

In March of 2013, I contacted the Winnemucca Museum and asked if they had any data supporting the story of red-haired giants. Their director informed me that although the skulls are robust, they are not considered giant. Also, the museum could no longer display the skulls because they are Native American and the museum could lose its funding. She also gave me a report from the BLM (Bureau of Land Management) which stated that the story of red-haired giants from the Lovelock cave was a myth… no giant bones were found, and explained that their red hair had been dyed.

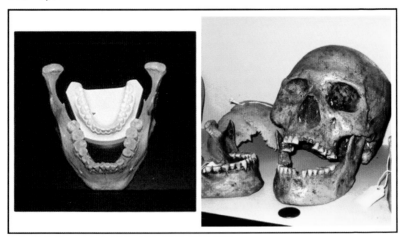

Winnemucca Museum photo by Stan Nielsen

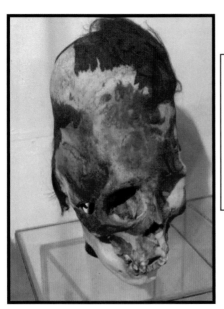

This non-human elongated skull in Paracas, Peru, had naturally red hair—straight from the mummified remains. Could there be a connection with the red-haired giants reportedly found in Nevada?

It may be that the red-haired giants were just a myth, but one might note that the BLM is a government agency, and as mentioned the museum could lose its funding if they continued to display those skulls. To produce a red-haired offspring it takes a recessive gene in both parents and only about one and a half to two percent of the population have red hair. Is the issue of red hair important? Yes, it very well could be. Red hair was non-existent in Natives of the Americans. Were Sarah Winnemucca's' writings erroneous? Would a whole tribe dye their hair red? A red-haired, non-human skull is on display in Paracas, Peru.

In 1895, miners working near Bridlevale Falls in Yosemite Valley, California, discovered the tomb of a woman with a child. The Martindale Mummies were acquired by Ripley's in February 1898 from Dr. Larry Cartmell and were first displayed in Scranton, Kansas, in 1899. The men who analyzed the remains suggested the height of six feet eight inches tall in death must have represented an actual height in life of about seven feet or more. If the height relationship between men and women was approximately what it is today, then the males of the species could possibly have been some eight feet tall. The origin of the Martindale Mummies remains a mystery.

In 1965, while leading a group of Boy Scouts into Hemlock Crossing on the Stanislaus River in the High Sierra Mountains of California, Dr. Robert Denton of Bishop, CA, found a huge human-like skull. The artifact, known as the Minaret Skull, found its way to UCLA where it was mysteriously lost. In 1977, after Al Berry interviewed Dr. Denton, he and I, along with another man, rode horseback into this area and started digging for more bones. The trip was very memorable, with excellent weather, and the horses did great. But the only significant things we found were blisters on our hands the next day.

Martindale Mummy

It seems easy to link the Martindale Mummies found in Yosemite, the bones of once seen but now missing red-haired giants in Nevada, with the Minaret Skull in the Sierras. Our puzzle begins to take shape and I think these, collectively, are a sign that enormous people have lived in and around the Sierra Nevada Mountains. These finds are not very far from where several sightings of Bigfoot have occurred and where I and others recorded hours of these creatures' vocalizations. So, why would it be difficult for modern humans to believe that giants could still be around... because they don't get to see one of these creatures firsthand. Is our government hiding artifacts that could be revealing? If so, why?

Jim Vieira is known for his research into the history of giants in the United States. In 2013, I had the privilege of speaking with him at a convention in Georgia. Vieira has compiled thousands of accounts of giant skeleton reports from the *New York Times, Smithsonian Ethnology Reports, American Antiquarian, Scientific American* as well as town and county history archives to make the case that the story of our past has not only been deliberately covered up, but is vastly different from what we are told.

The intent of this story is to expose the reader to reported history, much of it in and around the Sierras, and also to my experiences. But I want to encourage the reader to keep an open mind when considering these giants.

Several books have inspired me, including, but definitely not limited to, the accounts of miracles, giants, and cross-breeding mentioned in the Bible. In order for God to be God, it seems He'd have to stay within the rules that He established ("His word never changes," Mal 3:6). So, I figured, if all this was true, there must be a "type" of science behind some of those stories.

Then, *Quantum Enigma*, by Bruce Rosenblum and Fred Kuttner caught my attention. This is a good book for those interested in trying to unlock and understand some of the mysteries that we are confronted with today. Could quantum physics be the vehicle that brings answers to some of anomalies behind these forest giants that seem to appear and disappear at will?

Chapter 19

Peru

(Enigmas associated with Bigfoot?)

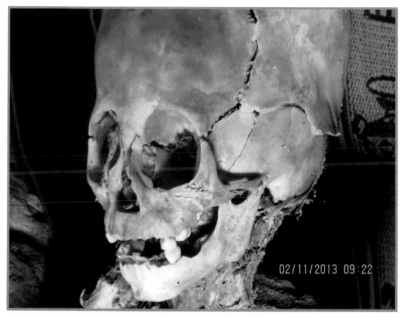

02/11/2013 09:22

The skull above was unearthed just outside Wayqui, Peru. Archeologists determined the mummified remains are not human. Myths and legends of many different cultures include monsters of humanlike appearance but with exceptional size and strength.

In February of 2013, I went to Peru for two weeks and was privileged to be in the company of five outstanding men. Professor **Judd Burton**, anthropologist, author and teacher. **Joe Taylor**, author and fossil casing expert. **Brian Foerster**, author and biologist. **Richard Shaw**, producer, director and film maker. **L.A. Marzulli**, author/researcher, lecturer, biblical scholar and chronicler of the Watchers DVD series. We went there in hopes to understand more about the pre-Inca people, the enigmas surrounding elongated skulls, and the puzzling megaliths that claim much of South America. Because of my vocal interaction with Bigfoot, or what some say could be the biblical Nephilim, I was interviewed by Mr. Marzulli and consequently invited to join the expedition. Could Bigfoot's sagittal crest (elongated skull), their humongous size, and their intelligence have any connection with the enigmas in Peru?

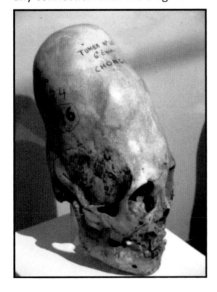

Chongos non-human skull, at the Ica Museum in Peru, 200 miles south of Lima

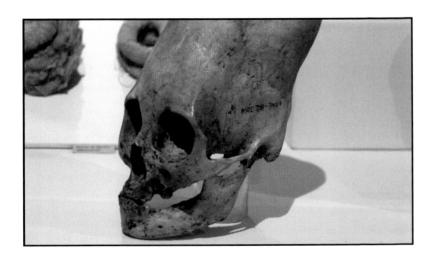

Peru captivated us for two weeks...we were filming it all. After visiting museums in Lima, the six of us traveled four hours south to the coastal town of Paracas. Dr. Burton analyzed several skulls, thoroughly documenting the sizes and weight — we wanted to know if they were of human origin or possibly non-human. Many of the skulls were definitely human, some elongated skulls were the product of cranial deformation (cradle-boarding), but some show no signs of the skull having been purposely altered, i.e., cradle-boarded. In fact, those skulls did not have two parietal lobes, like we do...no evidence of a sagittal suture. In the distant past could these elongated skulls have belonged to a culture that was associated with the construction of the enigmatic megaliths, mostly seen in the higher regions of Peru?

In Cusco, the Inca hub, we acclimated to the 11,000 + feet in altitude, and then drove cross-country hundreds of miles to several other areas of interest. Throughout Peru we witnessed megalithic rock formations that were pre-Inca. The method used to move those enormous stones from a quarry over 40 miles away, up high onto a mountain, and fit them perfectly together was unfathomable. We also witnessed several other skulls that were innately elongated. But was there a connection with the elongated skulls and how these huge megalithic stones, some over 100 tons, got placed on these mountains? And how did this culture fit them so curiously and so perfectly together...using no mortar? Just as important to us was WHY? Is there an underlying story behind all this?

Cusco, Peru

Sacsayhuaman, Peru

We were told by museum curators that many of the ancient artifacts, e.g., elongated skulls and giant bones were kept locked up by the government. Could the artifacts found in South America have anything to do with these current-day giants in the North, who they might be and where they may have come from? Could they be associated with the giants that are mentioned in Greek mythology and biblical accounts?

After personally seeing these megaliths and the unusual skulls I became convinced that at one time there was a culture on earth that had advanced technology...certainly more than we have today. Biblical accounts mention a race of beings (pre-flood) that had abilities beyond ours...they have been referred to as the *Fallen Ones*, the sons of God. And they created giants.

But, who and what were these Fallen Ones? Celestial beings (angles) that came to earth and mated with human women: their offspring were giants called the Nephilim (Gen 6:4—pre-Flood, and Num 13:33—post-Flood). Could Bigfoot be a Nephilim, or a remnant of one? If so, could they have attributes that are superhuman? Something superhuman with amazing technology was responsible for what I saw in Peru, and also the enigmas associated with Bigfoot that I witnessed in the Sierra Nevada Mountains of California. Supposedly, thousands of years ago, advanced technology was shared with humans by celestial beings (the *Fallen Ones*) in exchange for sex with earthly women...what a deal. We humans got a kick-start on technology and the aliens got sex. Was that a good trade or could there have been another "sinister" reason behind it all?

Because man had broken away from his creator by this deception from the Fallen Ones, God made those aliens a promise. He would bring back His creation (humans) to their original state, i.e. total oneness with Him (Gen: 3:15). With all this going on, how was that going to happen? God needed to talk to his peoples' ears—our spirit was separated.

Genetic manipulations by alien beings were becoming wide-spread, but not just in humans, in animals too. Bizarre entities were being created, thus begetting Greek and Hebrew mythologies. Only one human family had not been influenced by DNA manipulation and was saved from an earthly disaster, which destroyed these unusual creatures, also destroying the Nephilim. But, celestial beings against God were not giving up; they came again, and for the next 400 years cleverly wiggled into humanity... setting the stage for a huge spiritual war; the hybrids were here again.

The above statement may sound religious or idealistic to many and if a closed-minded classical scientist even got through that paragraph he or she probably dismissed it immediately; accepting that statement or perhaps adopting any of it as part of their professional life could put their tenure in jeopardy. I'm fairly sure politics and concerns about tenure may keep some professionals from being what they'd personally like to be and doing what they think they'd like to do. I believe more would get inspired if they personally witnessed the enigmas in Peru firsthand. At the very least they would surely scratch their head a little. For me, it took those biblical stories along with those Greek myths to put everything in a context that I could actually wrap my head around and put my hands on. My search for answers to the Bigfoot phenomenon may have taken a "giant" leap forward.

Historical artifacts suggest that many myths, legends and folklore may have begun from a seed of truth. Many biblical accounts are believed to be metaphors, and may serve the reader as such. Much more about the Nephilim and giants can be found in the Book of Enoch (not canonized), which in 1773 resurfaced in Ethiopia. In 1821, it was translated into English by Dr. Richard Laurence. Enoch goes into great detail regarding the relationship between humans and angels, and the giants they created. In Greek mythology these relationships were taken for granted—and Greek gods were giants. Like the biblical Nephilim, they were a product of celestial intervention into humanity—a hybrid.

The Greek god Zeus was famous for his many affairs, Hades was known for mining minerals from the earth, and Poseidon created a variety of unusual animals. When I suggest that Greek mythologies may have begun with a core of truth, some folks are just not havin' it. Many continually embrace their theology and tradition, and just aren't about to turn loose of them. Are we humans stuck in a self-imposed paradigm?

What does it mean to be human? To be human is identified by a highly developed brain that confers advanced skills in abstract reasoning, articulate language, self-awareness, problem solving, and sapience. Humans are bipedal primates and have an erect carriage, (Biology online). What adaptation in hominids caused us to be rational and self-aware? Did our cognizance really evolve? Is there an answer that includes God, but still has a scientific base? Perhaps raising classical sciences' disciplinary bar, yet acceptable to the many people that ascribe to the paranormal? Is it incomprehensible to challenge Darwin's theory of evolution? This is really thin ice.

Physicists worldwide accept it, one third of our economy depends on it, and it is undisputed; it's Quantum Mechanics. Quantum physics is a subset of quantum mechanics. Quantum physics challenges our perception of reality and is therefore very difficult to explain—not the enigma but how our consciousness encounters it. Nothing is real until it's observed...huh? How does one explain the unexplainable? This type of science is strange to most of us, but it is a certainty that commands our consideration.

We humans live in a three dimensional quasi-reality world (four if we include time). Quantum physics says there are more—other dimensions, possible parallel universes; we just don't access them in our current macro-world compulsory environment. Everything we try to imagine has its beginning and its end. But, how can we imagine the end of outer space—a wall, more space, what? If it has no end, how could it have had a beginning—Bang Bang?

Ever had a déjà vu? The literal meaning is "already seen." Those who have experienced the feeling describe it as an overwhelming sense of familiarity with something that shouldn't be familiar at all. Could our minds be attempting to link into another dimension? A dimension unrestricted by what we call "time?" Our intentional access to other dimensions seems inadequate, but is it really? Answers to challenging questions and issues seem to come to us when we're in a relaxed, non-analytical, state of mind and unchallenged by daily matters. Are we keeping ourselves separated from an inter-source that knows everything and can communicate with us when we are at peace? Could this state of being be the phenomenon that many call a spiritual experience, and be a form of communication with God? Could it be what Christians refer to as being saved, being one with God? What's in our way? Could it be ourselves believing we are separated from an inter presence that really knows all, unrestricted by time?

Have I gone too far with this? I'm not a preacher or a physicist but spirituality and quantum physics just might have something to do with these giants that seem to have some unique abilities. Could they actually alter the accepted macro-world of classical science and entangle it with the established unseen micro-world of quantum physics?

A life-changing experience began with me in 1971 and I still reach for answers. Perhaps it's so I could write this story and state these ideas. But what does Bigfoot want to say? I've got to know. What is the underlying meaning of them interacting with me and the others guys in that camp? My other remaining questions are: Could they just be a left-over mistake by the ancients? Were they genetically made for a specific purpose...a purpose yet to be known? Are they trying to trick me... who am I? Could they be the Nephilim?

Or, for the sake of open-mindedness, the answer could be that a conspiratorial group of six-to-ten-foot-tall techie humans are running around in the woods dressed in hair suits with huge homemade board feet pretending to be Bigfoot.

Perhaps I'm all wet and they are just an undiscovered ape of some kind. And all the people that claim they've seen one disappear are completely mistaken. And all the folks that claim Bigfoot is associated with UFOs are just screwed up. Scientists' DNA analysis is ridiculous, just pseudoscience... they can't be half human. These things can't talk...the Sierra Sounds and those guys, along with those professors, must have been smokin' some funny stuff.

*An exhaustive account of giants, and more on the enigmas in Peru, can be reviewed in Joe Taylor's book, Giants Against Evolution. It's a good giant compendium and an interesting read.

Chapter 20

DNA (Deoxyribonucleic Acid)

Today scientists are able to change animals' genetic makeup by altering the nuclear DNA in their bodies. If it can be done now in animals, could this technology have been used before on a higher level, by an advanced culture? Is it possible that Bigfoot is the result, or a remnant of that result? Many researchers think these entities are an undiscovered great ape, the missing link, and to properly expose them we need more infra-red and thermal imaging devices mounted to trees in the forest. Thus far the only parties that have profited from this are the companies that make those cameras.

As we give this very popular "ape" idea its due diligence, the Gigantopithcus blacki theory is the most popular view held. It's easy to jump onto that brain-train and accept Bigfoot as a leftover from Gigantopithcus; it would fit better into existing paradigms. Gigantopithecus is a reportedly extinct species, the remains of which have been found in Southeast Asia. It's been suggested by some scientists that Gigantopithcus stand upright and did not become extinct; an adult would be ten to twelve foot tall. Unfortunately, no DNA from those remains has been obtainable.

What about DNA from a Bigfoot? Would it be accepted as proof, even without a body? Can established scientists actually accept something so extraordinary and out-of-the-box? Or, might they stubbornly ignore evidence that licks its chops right before their eyes.

In November of 2012, Dr. Melba Ketchum unloaded a bombshell on the scientific community. After five years of delving into over 100 organic samples coming from purported Bigfoot, she joined the prestigious group of professionals that have stuck their necks out. She, along with a few others, will go down in history. But how will she go down? Most of the time when you're the lead "DNA wagon" you will get the first arrow.

The following excerpts are from Dr. Ketchum's interview. She is the owner of DNA Diagnostics and stated the following:

> "A team of eleven scientists with expertise in genetics, forensics, pathology, biochemistry and biophysics has sequenced three whole nuclear genomes from a novel, contemporary species of hominin in North America. The mitochondrial DNA was fully modern Homo sapiens sapiens indicating that the species is a hybrid cross between

modern Homo sapiens in the maternal lineage and an unknown hominin male progenitor."

- Melba Ketchum, D.V.M. and Owner, DNA Diagnostics

Dr. Ketchum went on to say that the hybrid combination of a human female and an unknown male primate first emerged some 13,000 to 15,000 years ago. Dr. Ketchum says that Sasquatch is a "type of person," an elusive distant cousin of the human race that has been living almost invisibly "under the noses of humans" for millennia as it has stuck to the most remote parts of the world - perhaps even underground for shelter - trying to avoid human populations.

Dr. Ketchum's analysis threw a curve in Gigantopithcus blackist folks, unless, of course, Gigantopithcus were fellow members of the genus Homo. The definition of "sapiens" is "to be wise." Is Bigfoot wise? Yes, the ones I dealt with were smart and seemed to figure out what we were doing, and didn't fall into any of our camera traps. We did, however, capture hours of vocalizations on cassette recorders over a period of several years.

According to Dr. Ketchum the maternal side of Bigfoot is 100% human. Perhaps we need to consider carefully the core of what the nuclear (father) side could be. Based on the factual evidence available and anecdotal data I've pulled out, which was mentioned in the previous chapter, along with my personal experiences, my brainwave of what this being may be gets freakier.

Obviously, the reader can stick with classical science and keep looking for that elusive ape running around in the woods. Or maybe entertain the biblical accounts of celestial beings (angels, as some would have it) co-mingling with humans, and at the time give a little consideration to the different mythologies that speak of unusual animals and remarkable giants.

Hopefully I've opened up a mind or two to possibilities and found a suggestive common denominator that answers some questions? Maybe entertain a thought that would test our "assumed" reality of how we've been trained to think this world really works and how humans really evolved?

Chapter 21

Closing Thoughts

Whether or not Bigfoot is anything other than an undocumented great ape is yet to be known. Whatever these creatures are, they are obviously unique. Bigfoot has consciously decided to inhabit the wild, rarely interact with so-called 'civilized' humans, and they have no reason to become like us. These beings do, however, seem to find us interesting and observe what we do. To prevent exposure, utilizing their flexible vocal mechanism, they have become experts at diversion and mimicry. They have restricted our exploitation and adapted a life of stealth; occasionally being seen, but more often, just peering through the dense forest and observing our behavior - probably wondering why we are so inept with nature. Very similar, I think, to how the Native Americans used to be. They have many stories that refer to hairy giants.

Every account I have regarding Native lore accepts Bigfoot without any reservations (no pun intended). I had the privilege of interviewing a Native American who finally opened up to me and began to answer a few questions. One was what he thought these creatures were and what was their purpose? His answer has always stuck with me. "They are here to help us," he said. Native Americans have spiritual guides, which are adopted by them for the purpose of helping to get through catastrophic events. Why? Because animals make it through those horrific times and humans don't do so well. Many Natives have a Bigfoot as their spiritual guide.

Native American lore also speaks of these hairy giants vocalizing from the forest, like a baby's cry. That cry would compel a woman to look for the source - then...the woman is gone. Could their stories of women being abducted be true? In the past could there have been cross-breeding with the natives, thus creating a subspecies? Would the laws of genetics allow this? These beings would have to be very, very closely related to humans for this to happen. But, what would account for the different shapes of footprints, their different types of vocalizations, and the different accounts of human-like facial features? Many report a sagittal crest. But, some reports say no sagittal crest.

The tracks we cast in the Sierras were 'splayed', five-toed prints. The Patterson prints were narrow, more human-like, with a defined arch. Most recordings from a purported Bigfoot are of a scream or yell of some type. The family of giants around our Sierra camp chattered among themselves, very much like the account given to John Green in his interview with Albert Ostman. The detailed account of his alleged 1924 abduction by a Bigfoot is very compelling and can be found in Green's book *Sasquatch, The Apes Among Us*. In his account, Ostman called them *people*. He also said they were "continually chattering". Are they people?

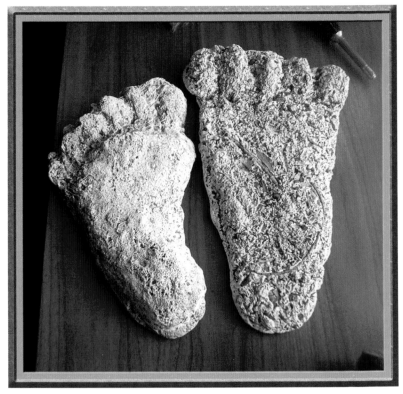

Left: 6 toes, 15" track found in the Sierras / Right: 18" track Sierra Camp

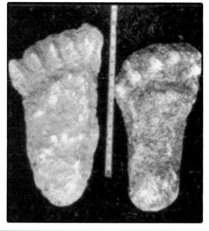

Left: Bluff Creek / Right: Buckey tracks from Shasta County, CA

More often than not we researchers put folks aside when they say that Bigfoot is not an ape, but are a type of people (technically speaking we are all apes). Sometimes folks insist that these entities are paranormal, that they saw one disappear, and most of the time, their account is dismissed and completely discredited. However, to me there was no logical explanation when at different times some very unusual, unexplainable sounds occurred at our camp. Many folks report tracks that suddenly stop with no sign of where the tracks could have gone, where they came from, or how they even got there in the first place. Are all these accounts contrived or could they have just been mistakenly construed?

The analysis of the recordings captured in the Sierras gives insight into the nature of these elusive beings. I've always wanted to know what they were saying to me. But, the only way we will ever know exactly what they want to communicate is if one points to a tree and says, "Ouga." If he points to two trees and says, "Ouga, Ouga," perhaps he means two trees. The more interaction we can encourage, the more we can begin to learn about them.

There are many things we humans still need to absorb about nature and the cosmos. Humans, who assume superiority, arrogantly attempt to conquer and challenge nature instead of living with it. We seem tempted to redefine conceivably valuable Bigfoot reports, and keep those unusual, strange and out-of-our-paradigm claims in a closet. How will we ever learn without opening our minds and pulling ourselves out of traditional thinking?

My story establishes that meaningful interaction can be made with these giants. If you want, call them people, or great apes, or remnants of demigods - you can make that choice. Whatever they are, it would be good if we could communicate with them. We need to be aware of their uniqueness and be mindful that this particular hominid has a great deal of intelligence - maybe even has the ability to exploit "quantum laws" that humans haven't learned to access yet (or maybe became recessive in us). They seem to have all the instinctual ability of an animal, but also possess a developed level of intelligence and, who knows, possibly much more. And, it's possible that there may be different types of these entities stealthily holding up in the backwoods.

While remaining within the scientific disciplines, but remaining spiritually open-minded, I suggest those curious scientists step up, stick their neck out, and join the ranks of men and women whose names will be remembered after passing on. Collectively, with dedicated hominologists and serious researchers, we can *maybe* get this discovery done. We should *not* get defensive, share our knowledge, and get it together? I'm in.

Lake Tahoe, Sierra Nevada Mountains

Bill McDowell w/ Eagle and his mules

Epilogue

Warren Johnson peacefully passed away in his home on April 30, 2011. During hunting season that September, Larry and David Johnson (Warren's two sons), along with his grandson, Jeff, took Warren's ashes to the camp and spread them around that beautiful high-country forest he so loved. Warren always said that this area was as close to God and heaven as he could imagine. As pristine as this area is, I guess now he may know of a place that's even better.

Louis Johnson and Bill McDowell have not hunted at this camp in years and don't seem to want to be involved in researching the mysteries it still holds. Although my interest in the location is to learn more of its curious inhabitants, the younger Johnsons still considered this camp their get-away-from-it-all spot – they hunt deer and want this area to remain unspoiled as long as possible.

Al Berry passed away on January 30, 2012 at his home in Carmichael, California. His last visit to the camp was in the late 90's. He retired from the State of California as a geologist and spent much of his last years writing. His most recent book, entitled *XO*, was released in 2011 and is about his experiences as an officer in Vietnam. Al was a close personal friend. We explored a lot of country together, and he is sorely missed.

Peter Byrne lives in Pacific City, Oregon, and devotes most of his time searching that area for signs of these creatures. We both admit that we don't know what they are yet and we differ on the approach, but we're both actively seeking that answer. Peter is still very busy writing books and heads to Nepal each winter.

My horses are still on my ranch in California, eating hay every day and processing it out the next, but, hopefully waiting for another adventure with me. I am the only one of the original hunting group still actively engaged in the search of this unknown.

The trip to this area is difficult, not for the weak of heart or anyone without a strong constitution. Some of the guys from the original group think that Bigfoot should be left alone. But, I, along with other devotees, just can't let the Bigfoot mystery lie. There is an answer and it's in my make-up to seek it out.

About The Author

Ron Morehead is an *adventurist*, a positive *someone* who loves life, but often lives it on the edge. As a SCUBA diver, he swam with the hammerhead sharks, has been filmed in *Mexico's Pacific Ocean* riding the backs of giant manta rays, and been a safety diver for the filming of Right whales in *Patagonia*.

As a private pilot, Ron has flown his own aircraft from the Alaskan bush to the Costa Rican jungle. Besides travelling to the ancient Mayan civilizations in the Yucatan, he has also flown into a remote jungle area of Chiapas (Southern Mexico) on an anonymous Mayan discovery expedition. What he saw was thought to be one of the last remaining strong-holds of the Mayan people. He has ventured into Western Nepal's Suklaphanta Wildlife Reserve to help assess the tiger population, explored the jungles of Bardiya on elephants, and been in the wilderness of Siberia looking for evidence of the Russian Yeti.

In 2013 he ventured into Peru to investigate the mystery of elongated skulls and the enigmatic structures associated with the pre-Inca people.

Over the years Ron has been interviewed by several radio programs and has been televised by the BBC and other learning channels. He was a guest speaker at the Darwin Museum in Moscow (Russia) and for years he has given presentations at symposiums and conferences about his Bigfoot/Sasquatch experiences. He has openly shared his knowledge and accounts with others. His book, **Voices in the Wilderness,** chronicles his 40 years of researching the enigma. He produced 2 CDs with actual Bigfoot vocalizations, focusing on the interaction he and others had with these forest giants.

As a successful businessman, and a father of four, his entrepreneurism has afforded him the time and means to do many things. He doesn't consider himself an active participant in a man-made religion, but is deeply spiritual, and yet he can be a classic *bad boy*. Besides being a gifted entertainer-musician, his incredible life as a speaker has taken him worldwide.

Unlike most of our culture, Ron has learned to live with nature on its terms and not attempt to conquer it. His story about Bigfoot/Sasquatch is a chronicle that has drawn much attention over the last 40 years. It's a true story and he says that it's been the biggest adventure of his lifetime.

As an independent and free spirit, Ron (my dad) has had, and is still having, a remarkable life – anything but ordinary – that's for sure.

Rachelle (Morehead) Araque, daughter

Sierra Deer Camp Investigation

By Joe Hauser

Certified Arborist #WC5390
Certified Utility Specialist #WC5390U
California Workers Compensation Claims Management Specialist
Primitive Living Skills and Outdoor Survival Instructor
Member of Western Chapter of the International Society Arboriculture

Education:

B.Sc, Biology, San Diego State University, San Diego, CA
A.S. Degree, Applied Science, Imperial Valley Jr. College, El Centro, CA
Business Management, Sears Executive Management Institute, Chicago, IL

In 1971 reporter Al Berry recorded the sounds of an unidentified creature at a primitive deer hunting camp in the high Sierras of California. The sounds were believed to be that of what is commonly referred to as "Bigfoot" or "Sasquatch."   Researchers at Fauna Communications (http://www.animalvoice.com) asked me, to travel to the deer camp to investigate the possibility that the sounds were broadcast from speakers or some other amplifying device that had been concealed in the area where Berry had set up his recording equipment.

On September 28, 2003, myself and Ron Morehead backpacked into the remote deer camp and spent the better part of three days conducting this investigation. The following is the results of the investigation.

NOTE: Partly due to the detailed seven-page account of this area, the complete report has been omitted by the author; however, Mr. Hauser's conclusions are as follows:

- The mountain top and camp area is very remote and pristine in nature with little evidence that man is there other than in the deer hunting season of late summer and fall. Other than hunting there were no other recreational activities other than backpacking that could be done in the area. Also the camp is well off of any backpacking trail.

- Access to the camp is limited to foot or horseback and all supplies and equipment have to be hauled in up a very steep trail and along walk across country.

- The trail, the camp, the shelter, the microphone tree, the granite rocks, the spring, and the area around the camp were all consistent with the descriptions that Al and Ron had provided to me prior to backpacking into the camp.

- The primitive shelter was very impressive and had no evidence of a speaker, amplifying device, or speaker wire either on the inside or the outside.

- The ground and pine duff cover in an old growth forest is very static and even small disturbances like a squirrel digging a hole leaves a mark that lasts for many years to come. In digging into the ground around the microphone tree the fact that the pine duff and soil were evenly distributed with no signs of mixing would indicate that it had never been dug up to hide a speaker wire, speaker, or an amplifying device. The area around the whole camp and up to and behind the granite rocks west of the microphone tree showed no visible signs of disturbance by man. The only area that looked used by man was the camp itself and the spring.

124

• There was no evidence that a speaker, speaker wire, or an amplifying device had been hung from or secured to any of the trees that were in the area. There was also no evidence that any of the trees had been climbed to hide or conceal such devises. Also because of the nature and the size of the trees and the openness of the area it would have been nearly impossible to conceal a device in any tree.

• The granite rock outcropping west of the shelter and camp also showed no signs of disturbance and there was no evidence to indicate that a speaker, wire, or an amplifying device was ever hidden in that area. Do to the nature of the area it would have been nearly impossible to conceal a device without someone being able to see it.

• The remoteness of the area and lack of human interference is evidenced by the bear "bed" that was located very near the camp. This indicates to me that this animal does not perceive any threat from the camp except maybe for a short time during the hunting season.

• It is my opinion that the remoteness and wilderness state of the area would also help to keep an unidentified species isolated enough to not be discovered without extensive and long-term field work.

• The rocks that were out of place may have other logical explanations but if a species were using rocks to generate sound than they would have at least a casual knowledge of what rocks to us to accomplish this activity. Further evidence needs to be collected including the testing of rocks in the area and the sounds they produce as compared to sounds that have already been recorded.

Final Conclusion:

In my opinion there was no evidence to support the theory that a speaker or any amplifying device was used at the camp to create the sounds that Al and Ron had heard and recorded in 1971. I believe that based on this lack of evidence, the sounds recorded were of a yet unidentified species that inhabits this remote wilderness area.

125

Products

Click on the items below to go to our online store:

**Voices In The Wilderness
(2nd Edition)**
(Ebook)

The author, Ron Morehead, relates a progression of experiences that is quite compelling and very convincing. His story begins in 1971 and gives his 40-year chronicle. **Get the Ebook and take it with you where ever you go.**

The Bigfoot Recordings
A True High Sierra Wilderness Story

Volume 1 CD (right) is 40 minutes. Produced in 1996 by Ron Morehead features very clear vocalizations captured in 1972 by Alan Berry, the investigative reporter.

The Bigfoot Recordings Vol. 2

Volume 2 CD (left) is 40 minutes. Produced in 2003. Written, produced and narrated by Ron Morehead. It features rhythmic rapping-pounding sounds, and almost understandable phrases emanating from these creatures.

Click Here to go to our online store at
http://www.bigfootsounds.com/store

Notes:

Notes:

Notes:

Notes: